What People Are Saying About Synergy Energy!

"This book, *Synergy Energy*, is a way that will help build wealth by showing people that creating a partnership mindset can change their lives and expand their world. Networking and connecting with the right people is pivotal for success in business and life. These authors have jam - packed this book with great information that can ultimately make your dreams come true."

Marilyn French Hubbard, PhD
Author, *Sisters Are Cashing In: How Every Woman Can Make Her Financial Dreams Come True*
Founder of the National Association of Black Women Entrepreneurs, Inc. (NABWE), and Sr. VP & Chief Diversity Officer at Henry Ford Health Systems.

"Synergy Energy! True to its name... a masterful work of Pam Perry, combining the talents of its authors and that of the various principles contained within its pages. If adhered to, this book and the principles contained therein, will help your ability to lead with much greater power than if any of the individual principles were used alone."

Glenn R. Plummer
CEO — Christian Television Network
www.ctnusa.org

"Working together works is the ideology of this book; and it's a philosophy that is biblical. We can all stand a lesson in unity...especially now, when so many businesses and ministries are challenged because of the economic climate. In unity, there is strength...this book will strengthen your ministry!"

Dr. Teresa Hairston
Publisher/CEO of Gospel Today Magazine
www.GospelToday.com

"In a global marketplace, it is more important than ever that we realize what it takes to brand and market our products or services. Tap into the mind of marketing genius Pam Perry and read *Synergy Energy* for ultimate success."

Pastor Rudy Rasmus
St. John's United Methodist Church in Houston
Author of *TOUCH: Pressing Against the Wounds of a Broken World*
www.Touch1.org

"Pam Perry is one of the most focused communicators in our country -- a talent that was born from her remarkable ability to connect people for their positive and mutual benefit. It's what we used to call networking, but it's Pam's way of bringing purpose to promotion. When you see how seamlessly Pam weaves her skills of promotion and networking, you'll see how her winning formula will create winning partnerships for you. And that's what synergy is all about!"

Helen Love
Producer with Detroit Area on Aging and Community Relations Executive

"There is only *One* word for Mrs. Pam Perry and that is Marketer; she knows how to make sure that you or your vision is at the right place and known by the right people to get the right and desired results."

Marilyn White
Publisher, Precious Times Magazine
www.precioustimesmag.com

"Pam is a protégé of mine who just loves to pull together PR projects for ministries and coach Christian authors. She's always been about THE MESSAGE. Though she is working in the ministry arena – don't get it twisted – she brings a high level of her public relations energy, contacts and relentless internet promotion to get the buzz going like she's working for one of the 'rich and famous' celebrities or well-known brands. She's done that too – but she's in the space now to raise the bar for Christian authors and ministries. Read this book and learn how to be branded from one of the nation's experts in the African American Christian market."

Terrie M. Williams
Author *Black Pain: It Just Looks Like We're Not Hurting*
President, The Terrie Williams Agency
Founder, Healing Starts With Us Movement
www.healingstartswithus.net

"A lot of people have a lot to say about things they don't know a lot about. They make a lot of money talking a lot about theories, and people pay good money to hear their motivating stories. But it all evaporates when they leave the seminar, because there's no substance to the content. It's hard to find authors or seminar leaders who actually care about their audience and readers, while having the ability to deliver real information that will make a radical change when applied.

Anthony and Crystal Obey walk their talk. They live what they teach. They are the living proof that you can change your financial life by creating wealth with no money, no risk, and little time, through the use of Joint Ventures. After doing Joint Ventures and teaching people around the world to do the same for 22 years, I have seldom seen such power, integrity, and ability in any two people. I have yet to see them not deliver on any promise, fail at any goal, or shrink from any challenge. They are probably the best copywriters in the US, and they understand the very essence of Joint Ventures. Talk is cheap, and the proof of the pudding is in the eating. Well, Anthony and Crystal Obey make great Joint Venture pudding.

The Obeys are the DollarMakers Country Directors for the United States, as well as being DollarMakers Certified Business Mentors. I unreservedly endorse and recommend the teachings and training of this powerful young couple. Whether you have a business or not, and regardless of your background, education, circumstances, or age, Anthony and Crystal's new book, *Synergy Energy*, is the key to wealth, success, and happiness for you. Joint Ventures are the way to create financial freedom with no cost or risk, and very little time. This book is a valuable manual that is easy to understand, applicable to any situation, and to the point. No fluff – just real stuff, based on proven systems. If you only buy one book this year, this is the one you should be investing in; you'll be glad you did."

Robin J. Elliott
President, Elliott Enterprises Inc., Trading as DOLLARMAKERS

"Impactful, insightful and thought-provoking. Add to your reading library!"
Kevin Wayne Johnson
Author, Give God the Glory! series of books and devotionals
www.writingforthelord.com

"Pam Perry knows how to unleash the power of relational marketing and positive alliances to make big things happen. Recommended!"

Marilynn Griffith
Author of *Rhythms of Grace*
Founder of the SistahFaith Network, www.marilynngriffith.com

"Pam Perry is the connoisseur of creating connections, the maestro of marketing and princess of publicity - and she's in love with the Lord! From corporate professionals to committed pastors, Pam shares strategies to get your story out of you - and onto bookstore shelves and in newspapers, magazines, radio and television. This is a must read from Pam Perry - "the-publicity-how-to-guru!"

Angelo B. Henderson
Pulitzer Prize winner, writer, pastor, motivational speaker and radio talk show personality. www.angelohenderson.com

"Pam Perry is a public relations powerhouse! Her infinite energy and creative vision will instantly bedazzle you as she shares expertise about marketing. But what distinguishes Pam is her loving spirit and genuine kindness. She gives off a vibe—especially when she smiles—that makes you feel like angels are descending around you and your project, to lift them into a heavenly realm of success. Pam is phenomenal!"

Elizabeth Atkins
Author*Speaker*Journalist
www.elizabethatkins.com

"*Pam* is a ministry marketing maven on a mission to enlighten writers and business owners on the power of joint ventures and importance of branding for business and ministry. A must read for those determined to succeed!"

Sheri Clark Brooks
Filmmaker, Speaker, Author
25 Steps to Becoming a Star Writer & Screenwriting and *Filmmaking in 12 Steps*
Working to educate, promote and assist literary entrepreneurs
www.writerslegacy.org

How to Use the Power of Partnerships to Market Your Book, Grow Your Business and Brand Your Ministry

Pam Perry - Anthony & Crystal Obey
SynergyEnergyMarketing.com

Synergy Energy: How to Use the Power of Partnerships to Market Your Book, Grow Your Business, and Brand Your Ministry

Copyright © 2009 by Pam Perry and Anthony and Crystal Obey. All rights reserved under International Copyright Law.

Published by Perfect Storm Publications.

No part, including the cover, of this publication may be reproduced, stored in a retrieval system, or transmitted in any form or by any means, electronic, mechanical, photocopying, recording, scanning, or otherwise except as permitted under Section 107 or 108 of the 1976 United States Copyright Act, without either prior written permission of the Author.

Our books are distributed worldwide. Order our books via any bookstore or Amazon.com, Amazon.UK.com, BarnesandNoble.com or most any other bookseller.

For more information about Perfect Storm products, or publishing opportunities, visit our web site at www.perfectstormconsulting.com.

ISBN: 1-59268-090-9

Printed in the United States of America.

Cover Design By: Bob Ivory
IvoryCoastMedia.com

DEDICATION

*I dedicate this book (and everything I do) to God.
Without HIM, I am nothing.* **Pam**

*We thank God, our CEO and Counselor, for teaching us, leading us, and empowering us through adversity as well as accomplishment.
We also dedicate this book to two of our business mentors, Robin J. and Rika Elliott. Thank you for your kindness, your awesome vision, your valuable partnership, and your priceless example! You two are truly a God send!* **Anthony & Crystal**

FOREWORD

Pam Perry is a high-powered bundle of energy and information. When she speaks and writes people listen and read. Her marketing and public relations insights are not only very effective but empowering as well. Her spiritual based networking principles of sharing and partnering are right in line with what is needed in everything from small church ministries to large corporate entities.

Pam knows how to help people network for customers using marketing, public relations and a soft sell over the hard sell. I too am an advocate of the soft sell.

Soft selling entails getting information to identify problems in a friendly, conversational tone, then devising solutions using the ideas and information that you are willing to share.

Our mutual friend, Sonya, a graphic designer, describes her business as "helping to make people look good on paper." She spends her networking time brainstorming with her customers on how they can improve their business cards and other graphic images used to represent their firms. One of Sonya's favorite questions is, "If you could wave a magic wand, how would you enhance your graphic image today?" The answers often open up conversations that result in more business for Sonya. But she never presses, nor does she attempt to close a deal on the spot. She simply arranges for a more convenient time and place to expand the discussion and, ultimately, the size of the sale.

The key concept that Pam teaches us here is, when networking for business, never make the hard sell. Instead of trying to make money, solve problems and know that later, the cash will flow your way. Of course, it you find yourself giving away more than you are getting back, you might have to fine-tune your style of problem solving.

Thank you Pam for writing this gem of a book....a must read for anyone serious about succeeding in business.

George C. Fraser
Author: *Click: 10 Truths for building*
Extraordinary Relationships
frasernet.com

TABLE of CONTENTS

How to Create Synergy Energy for Your Book	15
Profits with Joint Ventures: What You've Been Missing	17
Networking with Real Power – From on High	19
How to Become a Joint Venture Broker and Why You Should	21
Before You Put Yourself "Out There"…Do You Have the Edge? Here's How to Get It	23
Your First Steps in Setting Up a Profitable Joint Venture Business	25
Taking Stock of Your Personal Image for Business	27
Strategies for Setting Up Solid Joint Ventures and Partnerships	29
What You Should Know About Branding Relative to Marketing	31
How to Become a Magnet for Lucrative Opportunities & Great Partners	33
What to Do Daily, Weekly, and Monthly to Brand Your Book	35
Where to Find All the Joint Venture Partners You Can Handle	37
Are You "Best Seller" Material? Ten Tips to Make "Best Seller" Status	39
How to Get Started Partnering For Profit Fast	41
Book Promotion "To Do" List Timeline	42
5 Quick and Easy Ways to Partner with Others to Reach Your Goals	45
Beyond the Book: Building A Platform	47
How to Maximize Sales and Minimize Costs with Barter	49
Bloggers and Blogging Can Create Publicity for Your Book	51
The Power of PR	55
Maximum Output – Minimum Time	57
How To Hire and Work with Your Publicist or PR Coach	59
How To Work From Home and Not Be Alone	62
How To Write a Press Release and Have It Do What It's Supposed To Do, Generate Buzz	64
How To Make Your Marriage Partnership Work	67
What Are Public Relations Retainers, PR Coaching, and Pay Per Placement Programs?	69
Joshua's Blueprint for Your Success…Revealed	72
Top 10 Tips For Free Publicity	74
How To Maximize Your Partnership With God	75

How To Get a Mentor and How To Be a Mentor	77
How To Flood Your Business with Eager Clients in Any Economy	79
How To Manage a Crisis and Position Yourself to Be an Expert	81
The Missing Link to Quickly Skyrocketing Your Sales…Guaranteed	83
Steps to Positioning/Branding Yourself in the African American Christian Market (AACM)	85
The Secret to Making Your Website Sell	87
Publicity Resources	89
Tools For a Successful Book Campaign	91
Publishing Self-Assessment	92
Listing of Christian Writer's Conferences	93
Essence Magazine Reporting Stores	99
Book Reviewer Contact Information	100
Recommended Reading for Authors	101
Recommended Books for Business Owners	102
Who Is Pam Perry?	103
How Can Pam Perry Help You?	104
Who Are Anthony and Crystal Obey?	105
How Can Anthony and Crystal Obey Help You?	106

INTRODUCTION

Are you ready to skyrocket the success of your career as a speaker, author, or recording artist, the growth of your ministry, or the sales and profits of your business by tapping into the tight-knit and loyal African American Christian market? Well congratulations!

If you're targeting the African American Christian market then this book is your foundational guide to reaching this market across three critical criteria which include...

1. Reaching as many African American Christians as possible (maximum people)
2. Reaching them as fast as possible (minimum time)
3. Reaching them with little to zero cost (with the least amount of money and other resources)!

That's right! This book is absolutely crammed full of little known marketing and partnership strategies that have transformed startup businesses into six and seven figure money-making machines in short order. Within these pages you will discover some of the hottest publicity strategies and techniques that have shot authors up the best-sellers lists' and recording artists to the top of the Gospel charts. You will learn how to position yourself in the African American Christian market to gain immediate credibility and attract the best opportunities. You will also get an introduction into one of the best-kept secrets of some of the world's top business gurus – the power of Joint Ventures, and how you can use Joint Ventures to quickly reach any goal.

Quite frankly, most people know very little about effective marketing or partnering, or even how important these concepts are to the growth of their organization. Sadly, that's the reason why many people fail to achieve the level of success they envision in this or any other niche. John C. Maxwell said it best, "If you want to achieve great success in business as a Christian then you need to be 'very very' Christian but also 'very very' business."

If you're a great Gospel singer and/or song writer, but you're not effectively promoted, you can still be overlooked, be a proverbial 'starving artist,' and ultimately fail. If you've got a great business concept the African American Christian market truly needs but you don't know how to reach them through effective marketing, you're doomed to mediocrity, frustration or worse – failure. And if you're striving to reach people with your ministry message and you're failing to employ the most proven marketing, positioning, publicity, and Joint Venture strategies, you're not reaching the full potential of your ministry.

The truth of the matter is this is exactly the plight of many thousands of entrepreneurs, authors, artists, speakers, pastors, and companies who are striving to reach the African American Christian market with their message, product, and/or service. You may feel like what you have to offer is truly worthy, timely, and even necessary; but if you lack the marketing savvy needed to quickly reach as many people in this market without overspending your budget, you'll never get your business or ministry off the ground.

"The Best-Kept Secrets of Effective Marketing and Partnerships... Finally Revealed!"

The GOOD NEWS for you is that now you have everything it takes to be extraordinarily successful in serving the African American Christian market with this book's blazing hot marketing, publicity, positioning, and Joint Venture strategies!

Now you will be able to reach tens or hundreds of thousands and even millions of people in this loyal market and gain an introductory understanding to some of the keys to generating significant profits, providing unique value, and building long-term success and sustainability. You must understand that it's not good enough to have great substance; you also need to have a great marketing, partnering, and publicity campaign if you want millions of African American Christians to know you, spend their dollars with you, and demand your products and services.

You will learn the value of building powerful partnerships and working with other people; but more importantly, you're going to discover specific strategies of *how* to work with other people and strike win/win deals. By working together and partnering with one another, we can reach all of our individual and collective goals faster, with less risk, and with far less effort. You're going to discover the best-kept secrets to forging lucrative and successful partnerships and Joint Ventures.

Getting Into this Book and Using it Correctly

Every section of this book is dripping wet with juicy strategies, tips and techniques that have made money and created success for those who've used them. We've structured this book as a workbook, a manual, a user's guide, or handbook – not just a 'book.' With this in mind, you can read this book all the way through if you like but you should definitely refer back to this 'handbook,' often, for specific insights that will help you as you implement one strategy and then the next.

You will find sections that help you maximize your relationships with God and people, your time, your money, and you'll learn how to better reach your goals. So refer to each section with the quick help of the table of contents when you come to a roadblock in your business, ministry, or career. You will be successful with the information contained in this book if you implement, learn more about, and eventually perfect each of the strategies taught.

So read some and then take MASSIVE ACTION on what you learn! We don't waste much time on theories or vague ideas; this is a book of concrete principles, strategies, tools, methods, and tips that will help you DO what you need to do to effective market, promote, and partnership your way to the top of the African American Christian market. So take action, massive action and you'll see just how effective these strategies are.

Be sure to claim the highly valuable FREE Gifts that we have for you at www.synergyenergymarketing.com and check for updates often. We're always striving to better serve you with much-needed products and services that will help you be more effective in marketing, promoting, and partnering for your business, ministry, or career.

The Synergy Energy Team
Pam Perry — Anthony and Crystal Obey

How to Create Synergy Energy for Your Book

By Pam Perry, Anthony & Crystal Obey

"Joining forces with others can bring big rewards." – Magic Johnson

Imagine being able to get your book into the hands of readers all over the world. Think about how much work it would take for you to access groups of people you have no connection with. What about the time it would take for you to get in front of people who never walk into bookstores, never visit the websites you market on, and who you have no idea how to reach.

You can eliminate these struggles by using joint ventures and being savvy with your book marketing strategies. You can touch more lives, educate more people, and yes, sell more books. You can sell more books faster, cheaper and easier when you really learn how to market them correctly. You can also have more fun while you build relationships with people who can turn into lifelong friends.

The cycle of success is weaved within the network of people you know. You have a dream - it's encased in the form of your book - now how do you create a team to make things happen as a new author?

The best marketing secret strategy to use is to create synergy with others. Authors must learn how to share information, experience and markets with other authors. Iron sharpens iron. Having a scarcity mentality brings scarcity into your life, while thinking abundantly brings abundance.

Partnering with others gives you opportunities that you could not have produced alone! You can get more buzz for your book by combining strengths and resources with others. A three-fold cord is not easily broken and there is safety in a multiple of counselors. In other words, you'll be safe and won't go broke if you learn how to cooperate with others and team up!

There are tons of ways to "joint venture" and partner with others if you're an author but make certain that the reason for forming the alliance is in SYNC with your goals, values and beliefs.

Here are some ideas:

1. Co-op a trade show booth with other authors. A booth at Book Expo America or CAABA (Christian African American Bookseller Association) could be out of range for an individual author but by coming together with other authors, the cost is just a fraction. This is win/win for everyone. The authors share the space and have a buddy who will "cover" them as they walk the exhibit floor and network with others.
2. Authors can partner with book clubs, bloggers, and radio station announcers by providing books through contests. This is often called a "trade for mention."
3. Do co-op mailings together with other authors to bookstores, libraries and church bookstores. This cuts down on postage. Mail postcards, book marks and sample books.
4. Authors can joint venture with entrepreneurs and nonprofits by providing free seminars or information that is important to their target market. Then the church or business can buy bulk copies of their products for the event. The author can also offer additional bonuses.
5. Do workshops or seminars with other authors. You both benefit by creating buzz to each other's audience and costs are cut in half (and the work too!)
6. Support other author's book releases. Go to their book signings; tell others about their new release via your blog, email, postcards/flyers at your own book table. The blessing will come back to you too!
7. Swap links with other author's websites, bookstores or media (this builds your traffic to your site and your Google rankings increase).

8. Trade excerpts with other authors and include that content in each other's E-Zine, E-Newsletter or blog. The more good content you give your market – the more they love you and support you.
9. Interview another author on a podcast or blogtalk radio show. Share media opportunities.
10. Do a virtual conference with several authors. Or host teleseminars together.
11. Do a swap with another author. Give away tip sheets or Mp3s as bonuses with book purchases.
12. Sell each other's books at your events. Offer a commission as an incentive so you make it financially worthwhile for others to promote your book.
13. Do a Membership site together on a topic that you and other authors are "experts" on. Take turns each month being the moderator or administrator. If it's a site for singles, parents or those who want life coaching, do the site together and provide valuable content to the members. They become your "fan" club and eagerly await your future products and services.
14. Bundle your book with another author in the same niche to create a special package for your readers. For example if your book is on weight loss bundle your book with another one on low fat foods. Bundle your prayer book with a DVD, or CD on prayer.
15. Bundle your book with an author in a complimentary niche. Put your personal finance book along with a working from home or retirement planning book.
16. Attend conferences together and get a group discount.
17. Share equipment. If you have a special camera, take promo photos for another author. They can let you use their specialized computer software.
18. Trade knowledge. If you know how to market your book to organizations and sell in bulk, show another author in exchange for their knowledge on how to market online.
19. Let non profit groups use your book as a fundraiser. Give them 50% of the price for their goal.
20. License out your material to deliver your book in other formats. Have someone read it on tape for an audio book. Have someone else create an online workshop for a targeted niche like moms, teens, leaders, etc. Partner with someone else to create other products like shirts, mugs, and hats. Let them create and sell the products while keeping a profitable piece of the income, and you collect a royalty.

As with any partnership, strategic alliances or joint venture, you need to do your homework to make sure it's a good fit. Remember your brand is on the line, so make sure you "click" with them and are just not trying to get your book out to their list or grab up their web traffic. Be sincere and ask will you enhance your brand by associating with them? And if so, what are you bringing to the table?

One of the best things about joint ventures is that the relationships you build can blossom into more projects, so you get the benefit of reaching your book goals while working with awesome people, and that makes your experience much more exciting.

By networking with others and adding synergistic partners to your "dream team," you will multiply your influence, impact and credibility – and your publishing career will soar to new heights. By helping others to succeed, you become a success also.

Profits with Joint Ventures: What You've Been Missing

By Anthony & Crystal Obey

"You can get anything you want out of life, if you're prepared to help enough other people get what they want."
Zig Ziglar

Our Joint Venture mentor and partner, Robin J. Elliott, is one of the world's top experts in using Joint Venture strategies in small to mid-sized businesses. He's helped tens of thousands of business owners around the world generate untold millions of dollars with little to no money invested, no risk involved, and very little time committed. You can literally create multiple streams of passive and growing income, quickly multiply your business sales, more easily reach the goals of growing an effective ministry, and accomplish virtually any goal with less personal effort by learning the Joint Venture strategies that we teach.

A Joint Venture is a win/win collaboration in which two or more people seek to achieve a common goal and share resources to get it done. It's nothing more than a partnership, strategic alliance, or win/win deal that is set up to benefit the common interests of all involved. Did you know that 20% of the revenues of Fortune 500 companies and the international 2,000 come from Joint Ventures; and 50% of those revenues are generated with competitors? Most of the CEO's interviewed said that they would lose their competitive edge if they stopped doing Joint Ventures.

So big businesses know how to create conglomerates, monopolies, and profit-making machines through Joint Ventures but the huge problem is that less than 2% of small to mid-sized business owners know how to use JV's in their business. Many of the world's top marketers and internet millionaires confess that Joint Ventures are one of their top secrets to making the majority of their profits, fast. "But how?" you may ask.

Let's Take a Deeper Look

Let's say you're starting your new business selling a hot new herbal product that'll shrink the user's waistline. You think your product would sell like hot cakes if you could just market it effectively.

There's one of two ways you can seek to market your product. Most people would buy ads, investing thousands of dollars into expensive advertising in newspapers, niche publications, pass out flyers, and even get real savvy and throw some money into Google Adwords. Four months later they've spent $10,000 and they've only made $1,000 back! This is the top reason most businesses fail to succeed. Bad marketing.

But wait a minute; you've been personally trained in using Joint Ventures strategies to start and grow your business with no money and no risk so you do searches online for 100 of the top herbal websites and webmasters who have an email list of at least 5,000 people. You collect their contact information, write a professional and persuasive email introducing yourself and how you believe you two can make some money while providing increased value to their database through your product.

Out of 100 potential partners, 15 people bite and agree to market your product to their list and split the profits 50/50. Within the next three months you sell $55,000 worth of product and net a cool $19,000 after the cost of goods sold and splitting the profits with your JV partners. Now you've got great partners who you can do more business with, you've got customers you can get repeat business from, and you've got profits in your pocket! And you did all this with no money, no risk, and very little time. You didn't even buy a shipment of product upfront - you had the product shipped straight from the manufacturer to the customer without any cash invested! Multiply that scenario by dozens and hundreds of times and you can catch a glimpse into how savvy entrepreneurs quickly build profitable businesses and multiple streams of income through Joint Ventures.

Joint Ventures give you unlimited resources and opportunities because they are founded upon the principle that says, "Whatever I need, someone else already has – all I need to do is provide enough value for them to Joint Venture with me."

All you need to do is approach people who have what you want with a deal that gives them what they want and you will strike endless Joint Venture deals. You have to study the people you want to collaborate with to learn what makes them tick, what their hot buttons are, and what they most care about. Do this so you can speak in the language of that person you want to work with, so you project that you're just like them, demonstrate that you're on the same 'page' as they are, and your goal is the same as theirs.

Look at how McDonalds Joint Ventures with the latest kids' movies to promote the movie and sell more Happy Meals by including that irresistible FREE toy. When I was a kid, I bought far too many kiddy meals for a FREE toy from my favorite kid movie. Look at how Burger King sells Pepsi products instead of becoming a bottling company. That's a Joint Venture. Look at all the companies and kiosks in Wal-Mart that become multi-million dollar companies overnight by Joint Venturing with the largest retailer in the world. You can fulfill all the basic needs and many of the wants of mankind in Wal-Mart. But they don't own it all; they've got great Joint Venture partners who provide great services and products.

You possess the power to literally get anything that you want out of life. There are dozens of specific Joint Venture strategies that we teach people to use that have generated billions of dollars and sadly, most people don't know how to use them. Creating win-win partnerships is all about leveraging other peoples' resources, time, experiences, platform, connections, money, database, equipment, infrastructure, list, and anything else you need to accomplish your goals. Most people get into business with a 'lone ranger' attitude and hit brick walls fast. We encourage you to learn more about Joint Venture strategies so that you learn how to create success with far less money, less risk, less suffering, less time, and less effort.

Networking with Real Power – From on HIGH!

By Pam Perry

"Whatever affects one directly, affects all indirectly. I can never be what I ought to be until you are what you ought to be. This is the interrelated structure of reality."
Martin Luther King, Jr.

I have always been wired to network. I love sharing information; connecting cool people with other cool people, seeing groups come together for a common cause. There's strength in numbers. Jesus said, *"I can of mine own self do nothing"* (John 5:30).

Because networking is so much a part of my personality, I have been teased a lot. I had even begun to think I was a bit strange – until I realized **Jesus was a networker**. He had to be. He took twelve folks and revolutionized the world. He turned it upside down!

He had a life-changing message that He imparted into mankind through the networking of men. The twelve disciples told some people, and they told some people, and so on and so on….

Isn't that what life is all about? No man is an island – we all need each other. How could anyone have received Jesus Christ as their Lord and Savior if they had not heard the Gospel? And how can they have heard without someone telling them? (Romans 10:14). That's the ultimate "network." Hooking people up to the "true vine" because Jesus said, *"apart from me you can do nothing"* (John 15:1 and 5).

Rev. Dr. Martin Luther King talked about networking too. He said, "As long as there is poverty in the world I can never be rich, even if I had a billion dollars…I can never be what I ought to be until you are what you ought to be. No individual or nation can stand out boasting of being independent. We are all interdependent."

Networking is not always about getting. It's really about giving. Actually, you're more blessed when you give than when you receive (Acts 20:35). I have a passion for God which has caused me to have compassion for people.

We must be committed to helping people. Ephesians 4:3 says, *"make every effort to keep the unity of the Spirit through the bond of peace."* When we network together, we weave a bond of ultimate power. Creating alliances and cultivating relationships is critical today, especially in business.

Networking is love in action (see 1 Corinthians 13). The master networker, best-selling author of *"Success Runs in Our Race"* and publisher of the Success Guide, George C. Fraser said, "I think success really involves the situations you get yourself into and the people you meet. No one can be successful by themselves – it's the relationships that you develop with the people around you. Throughout my life, I've had people who helped me do better."

Success does run in our race. Fraser has been on a mission to link African Americans together for the betterment of them all. For more than ten years, he has published *The Success Guide* to accomplish this goal. More than an upscale directory of contacts, it is the only vehicle that has African American professionals from 7 different countries and 75 cities. "It's networking in an instant with real people getting real results," said Fraser. He is also the author of the new book, "Click."

The Bible tells us in Matthew 25:39 to "love your neighbor as yourself." This is the key to a successful life. Another recurring phrase in the Bible is "one another." We are to: love, instruct, encourage, stir up, lift up, rejoice with, prefer, serve, pray with, submit to, admonish, minister to, fellowship with and edify ONE ANOTHER. Sounds like networking to me.

Nobody gets to the highest peaks without help from others. Networking is the identification of relationships for the purpose of sharing information and resources. Taking time for people and communication is the key. Don't ever get too busy to share information or your wisdom.

Success comes when you hook up with like-minded folks and kindred spirits. Moving ahead often involves reaching out and being willing to give. We reap what we sow.

So, how does one "network" for success? Here are some practical tips to implement:

1. **Be visible.** Dress sharp and snappy. Look like someone others want to know because your image says "success." Be willing to attend functions alone. Networking expands your circle of influence, builds your personal brand, and garners support.

2. **Give before you get.** Sow before you reap. Look for ways to be a blessing. Share information and resources with contacts before asking them for anything. Search for their interests and goals when meeting someone new. Figure out a way to help them.

3. **Gather, collect, and distribute info.** Position yourself as the "go to" person for ministry information. Provide regular updates about helpful events or books. Use an email database system like Constant Contact to simplify the process and send information attractively. See http://ministrymarketingsolutions.constantcontact.com.

4. **Write your vision.** Make it plain. Make the most of networking opportunities by having eye-catching marketing materials. Have more than a business card when going to a conference or event. Be intentional about your purpose. Have a bookmark or postcard describing your book. Offer a CD or brochure as a speaker.

5. **Demonstrate your sincere faith by being a person of character and integrity.** Follow the Golden Rule which says, "Treat others as you want to be treated", with respect and courtesy. Follow up and follow through. Deliver on your promises.

So be deliberate in creating partnerships, building relationships and keeping friendships. Make it your intent to be kind, really care about people, treat others with respect and value everyone.

If professionals work together, exchange ideas, contacts and learn how to joint venture – we'd really be about our Father's business and that's real power networking! By letting God direct and guide our actions, we'll have the ordained relationships for success and the "holy hook ups' to fulfill our destiny for the Kingdom.

Get Your Free Gifts Available at SynergyEnergyMarketing.com

How to Become a Joint Venture Broker and Why You Should

By Anthony & Crystal Obey

"I would rather earn 1% of the efforts of 100 men than 100% of the efforts of 1 man." **Paul Getty**

If you're a smart, bottom-line person who wants to be in business to make money, and not just money but maximum net profits from multiple streams, in multiple industries, and even in multiple countries, then you're going to love being a Joint Venture Broker! What's more, you can build an unlimited income, get anything you want for free, and do it all with little to no money, risk, investment, and very little time per Joint Venture you set up! And here's my promise – if you work hard and long hours for the next 12 months, you can literally retire. (Retiring means having more passive income coming in than you need to live on.)

One of our top JV partners, Robin J. Elliott, is a Joint Venture master with 22 years of experience. He and his wonderful wife, Rika, generate massive monthly profits from multiple Joint Ventures that require no more than one hour a day to maintain! He makes passive income from multiple streams. Robin always exclaims, "Everybody works for me!" But Robin is also very quick to quote Zig Ziglar who says, "You can get anything you want out of life, if you're prepared to help enough other people get what they want."

You see, these two components work hand in hand. If you're willing to give enough people what they want then they won't mind working for you to give you what you want. There is an elite group of people who are doing business far differently than the traditional, old-school way that says you have to do one thing, be known for one occupation, and have one stream of income. You know how it was back in the olden days in those little towns where you had THE town pastor, THE town doctor, THE town sheriff, THE town grocer, THE town real estate agent, and so on. Most people still do business this way and that's why they're so adversely affected by economic downturns and changes.

Joint Venture Brokers Aren't Affected by an Economic Crisis because Their Income Streams are Diversified and can Add New Ones on a Whim!

If you've dumped your entire life into just one thing then you've got all your eggs in one basket hoping to become the next Bill Gates, Michael Dell, or Warren Buffet. That's not the smart way to plan on building your business income. Savvy business people take on the Robert Kiyosaki way to building wealth which says I'm going to make money in all four quadrants and through multiple sources and strategies.

For instance, let's say a barber shop owner wants to grow and make more money. He's got a nice looking shop in a nice area and does a great job but he's no good with marketing his business. You know two great sources of business for him so you say to the barber, "Would you be willing to pay me 20% of all the business I bring to you since it's business you would have never had and didn't have to advertise to get?" He says, "Sure, I'll pay you a cut (no pun intended) instead of placing those expensive ads in the newspaper that don't get me much for my money anyway!"

So you design 5,000 special flyers with your name and phone number at the bottom of each one that you pass out to guys at a local college nearby. You use your writing, selling, and promotional skill to make a local barbershop sound like the best place in town for college students to get their hair cut for a great price, fast service, and hair styling that the ladies will love. You also pass flyers out at a local gym where a lot of guys hang out at nearby; and several other 'guy-hangout spots.' Your phone starts ringing off the hook with dozens of guys wanting to know where to get their hair cut so you take their name and contact details so you can track each person you get, then you tell them to call the barber and let the barber know you referred them. Before you know it, you're making an extra $500 bucks a month without cutting a single head and your only cash outlay was some paper and ink. Your income grows every month from this one JV and so does your vision! Plus, you're a dream come true for the barber.

You take that same fundamental strategy, get more Joint Venture education to learn more sophisticated strategies, and do the same basic thing with beauty salons, restaurants, real estate agents, financial brokers, chiropractors, and cosmetic surgeons etc. Over the next year you can completely replace your household income and get a 100% raise and plan your early retirement! You don't own a business, you don't cut hair or bake cookies or mow lawns or any of that – you make money by connecting people with the things that they need and want. The essence of being a successful Joint Venture Broker is in understanding that you're a problem solver, not product seller.

Nevertheless, if you do own a business, you can use these same marketing strategies to multiply your business and even train individuals to use these strategies to send you more business. You can train an army of salespeople who don't get paid from you until they send you business.

The best part about being a Joint Venture Broker is that it doesn't take degrees, certificates, licenses, or mandatory training to be one and you don't answer to anybody. Nevertheless training is available and the more you learn the more money you'll make, the quicker you'll make it, the less headaches you'll have in making it, and so on. Plus, it helps to do business with people who are already on the same page as you.

That's why we're the directors of **DollarMakers USA** and that's what we help people do. Learn how to make money as a Joint Venture Broker and join the international club of people who do Joint Ventures together all over the world. (You can learn more at www.DollarMakersUSA.com)

Before You Put Yourself "Out There"… Do You Have the Edge? Here's How to Get it!

By Pam Perry

"You can tell more about a person by what he says about others than you can by what others say about him."
John Maxwell

If you really want to "get out there" – make sure your packaging is tight. Work on the outside packaging as well as the "inside package." If not, you'll be hiring a publicist to do crisis PR for you because you'll need someone to do reputation management. And it's harder to stop bad press than to create good press!

So, what is the Edge? It's that "IT" factor that propels success in life. Do you have it? People who have the Edge share a number of characteristics. They are successful, but never at the expense of others. They are people who genuinely love and care about others. They abide by the Golden Rule and excellence (not perfection) is their goal.

They are long-term survivors in the business world, which has a way of devouring its own. They survive because they maintain friends. Relationships are the key to their success. They know more than networking. They connect with others and click!

They keep these friends because they are loyal to them. Their networks invariably describe them, in glowing terms.

Here are some of the qualities that can help you develop the Edge – which is essential before any PR campaign is to begin.

1. DEPENDABILITY. Do what you say you will do. This can be tricky, because it involves a certain amount of self knowledge and self management. If you say you'll follow up by 9 a.m. Friday, you have to know what is feasible for you to be true to your word. How long will it take you to finish a project based on other things going on? You keep your schedule and know your work habits. .
Never say, "I can not" before you've tried.

2. TRUSTWORTHINESS. You may hear gossip, but you do not have to pass it along. Don't spread something that is confidential. If you get a reputation for discretion, everyone will confide in you and you will know everything that is going on, even if you do not talk about it.

3. RESPONSIBILITY. People with the Edge accept responsibility for their actions and don't blame others if they fail. They don't make excuses and freely give credit to their associates. They are quick to apologize when they are wrong. A great trait to have!

4. COMMUNICATION. Keep in touch. Call people back. Be a nice person and write short, friendly email or regular notes to stay in touch. If you are in contact with your network of friends and associates when things are going along fine for you – you'll see that they'll be there when you need them. Don't just reach out to people when you need a "favor." People know when they are being used.

5. GENEROSITY. Make a habit of being generous and kind. Do things for free without expecting a return for it. Volunteer. Give away information or small bits of advice. Pass along job leads and provide tips to those looking for a job. Look for opportunities to put people in touch with each other. Be known as a "go to" person. Someone who is a "giver" not a "taker."

If you recommend a friend for a job or give them a lead for some business, you have given that friend a tremendous compliment and you have earned some long-term loyalty.

Even though you sometimes must say no to a request, make sure in some way you are always saying yes. Here is one way to do it. Whenever you decide you can not do something, give a credible reason then offer to help in some other way: "I can not attend this event because I am right in the middle of this assignment, but I would give you another person who would be willing to go and they would really get a lot out of it."

6. COURTESY AND KINDNESS: If you can't pray about it – don't talk about. Speak well of people or do not speak at all. This includes people who have fired you, wronged you or spoken badly about you. This is really how to have the Edge! This will toughen you up and mold your humility.

Display good manner at all times, particularly with those who actively antagonize you. It will drive them absolutely crazy. It may also win them over. The Golden Rule at work – will yield Gold every time. Do unto others as you would want them to do unto you!

7. INTEGRITY AND ETHICS. If you can't do it in front of your child, then don't do. If it makes you uncomfortable or you feel a "ping" in your spirit – that's a sign that is telling you you've crossed the line and in a danger zone. Develop a standard of behavior you can live with. Let your conscience be your guide. Let peace rule. This means when you make a tough decision, you feel you have done the right thing, even if it hurts.

8. PERSISTENCE. No one is ever a success in life unless they know how to persist. This is probably the most single way to get the EDGE!

Victory is assured to those who endure – until the end. Almost everyone has one good idea, one good effort, one good impulse. People with the Edge prove themselves by repeatedly being willing to do what others will not. They are not quitters. They are relentless and will try every angle and research every opportunity – and because they are relationship driven – will enlist the help of their friends.

People with the Edge can get everyone in the boat rowing in the same direction.

Before you think a good photo, brochure, corporate logo, website and press kit will give you the Edge – think again. The Edge is takes time to develop. Character counts and it starts on the inside. It starts at home. It starts with a relationship with Jesus Christ.

No amount of PR can promote the right message if you don't have the right interior motives. It takes time to become that sharp, so you might as well start now: in business, you are only as good as your relationships – with God, Yourself and others.

Get Your Free Gifts Available at SynergyEnergyMarketing.com

Your First Steps in Setting Up a Profitable Joint Venture Business

By Anthony & Crystal Obey

"Opportunity is missed by most people because it is dressed in overalls and looks like work."
Thomas A. Edison

There's no better way to do business, in our opinion, than using Joint Ventures and building multiple streams of income in your business using this mindset. It's beautiful because if you take the time to develop your skills, you can just make money in various ways, in multiple industries, through multiple strategies, without needing a storefront, money, investment capital, employees, or anything! While many people are stressed about the economic crunch, Joint Venture Brokers are capitalizing on the opportunities because when some industries fall, others always rise and JV Brokers are able to move seamlessly into these markets to make money. You're never tied into, or married to one business. You're mobile, flexible, adaptable, and elusive as a Joint Venture Broker.

As a Joint Venture Broker you'll be able to take advantage of rising trends in the international, national, or your local economy because you'll know how to leverage the businesses, expertise, customer base, products, services, staff, and other resources of other people. All you really need is a strong understanding of Joint Ventures and your very own arsenal of proven strategies.

You see, we're no longer in the "Industrial Age" of business where the richest people were the ones who owned the most real estate, oil, steel, gold and other tangible assets and commodities; also including large manufacturing companies. We're now in the "Information Age" where people like Bill Gates are building multi-billion dollar empires with intangible, intellectual assets. There are enough tangible assets already built up so you can build your fortunes by leveraging these assets using Joint Venture strategies to help the people who own these assets maximize them and take a cut of the profits for your efforts.

Let me say this, it's true that you don't have to own a business in order to be a successful JV Broker, but you can. You can be an employee, own a business, be a professional, be a salesperson, be a network marketer or even a student and still make a lot of money.

Though you don't need a lot to become a high-earning Joint Venture Broker there are a few things that you can't do without if you want to be successful. Here are the steps you need to take to building your JV income streams.

Connect with the Right People

You will meet some people who feel threatened, intimidated, skeptical, or whatever when you approach them about putting together a partnership. You want to work with people who know the power of partnerships, have the same goals, and are good to work with. That's why the **DollarMakers Club** is perfect. Everybody in the club is already pre-disposed to wanting to work together to make money, everyone brings a wealth of various resources to the table, we're all learning the same things, and we're able to maintain a high standard of ethics and morale. (dollarmakersusa.com has more information about this club.) The point is that you want to work with people who understand the power and value of partnerships and working together to accomplish goals.

Do a 'Resource Audit' on Yourself

You need to take stock of everything that you have to offer; tangible and intangible assets. This includes your skills, talents, personal and business contacts, money, access, intelligence, and other valuable resources that may be the perfect solution to other peoples' problems. You may discover that you know two people have what each other needs. In that case you need to 'broker' a deal whereby you get paid on all business that's done between these two parties.

Get Training, Training and More Training

As I said earlier, this is the "Information Age" which means that it's what you know that can make you successful and your lack of knowledge will cause you to fail. That doesn't mean becoming a professional student and racking up college degrees, that's not what training is. Most people don't learn how to become wealthy and savvy business people from professors who spend all their time lecturing from textbooks.

We've had our richest training in business by rich business people who've been in the trenches and built themselves up from the bottom to the top. Most of these people don't become college professors; they teach through books, CD's, DVD's, home study courses, seminars, conferences, webinars, and through inner circle clubs. Our website is loaded with Joint Venture training tools to help you be successful in your business, ministry, and personal finances. Training means you're learning and doing - learning and implementing. The more training you get and the more you do and implement, the more money you'll make, the more successful you'll become.

Build Your Support Team

You've got to have a strong support system in whatever you do and that applies to being a successful Joint Venture Broker as well. You need people in your corner you can learn from, share ideas with, and take good advice from. You want to choose some people who are using partnerships themselves to reach their goals. You want to learn from people who are successful and savvy as well. Not everyone who is successful is savvy, and being a good Joint Venture Broker may be a complete joke to some successful people who just don't understand it. These people may have built their business using traditional methods that took years and years of blood, sweat, and tears to do, but now that they're successful, they can't see any other way to have built that success. These types of people will ridicule and look down on you so stay away from them.

A good example is being in a room full of successful doctors and surgeons and telling them you're a network marketer. They may say, "Oh…you doing pretty well with that stuff?" or, "Oh…what do you sell; vitamins and makeup?" Well these are just people who haven't been in a circle of multi millionaires who have all built massive fortunes in MLM businesses without spending half their life in college!

Take Massive Action!

This is the most important thing you can do. You've got to learn and do, learn and do, in order to be successful. You'll get small results if you make small efforts but you'll get massive results if you take massive action!

Taking Stock of Your Personal Image for Business

By Sherese Duncan

"Fashion fades, only style remains the same." **Coco Chanel**

The way you present yourself in business and everyday interactions is a powerful vehicle for promoting your company.

Whether you represent a small business or a major corporation, your goal is positive results with clients, both current and potential ones. But before you can get your foot in the door the first time—or the tenth time--your visual image has to be attractive to your prospect. Some people would disagree but it's true. You may be able to make the appointment over the phone, or sell tons of products online, but in person your first impression on your prospect is VISUAL.

Your image is made up of numerous elements, some you carefully cultivate and others you may not even be aware of. To give yourself an image "check up," there are several areas you can look at:

1. **Others' reactions to you**. Other people's initial reactions to you can tell you a lot about whether your image is working for you or against you. Ask yourself, do people assume you are a lot older or younger than you really are? Do people take you seriously, or do they seem unconvinced or dismissive? Are strangers surprised when you tell them what you do for a living?

Such questions should help you interpret signals you receive from different people in your various spheres of interaction. Also, are you changing your introduction based on the situation? You should be. This is important so that your not presenting a cookie-cutter approach which is very easy to pick up on.

2. **Your body language**. Sit if front of a full-length mirror. Study how you look. Be sure to examine all parts of your body. How do you look in different positions? Is your body saying what you want it to say? When you want to appear friendlier, are your arms folded? Are you sitting in a masculine position, when you want to look softer? Once you are aware of how you look, you can make little changes here and there to make your body say what you want it to say.

In business, the handshake is the ultimate body language. A limp handshake tells me your not very confident, but on the other hand an extremely tight handshake tells me you trying to hard. Make sure your handshake is nice, comfortable, and firm. Also, use the full hand instead of just shaking hands with your fingers. A good handshake is basic but it's very powerful.

3. **Your business approach**. Professionals today need to know the new rules in business. In life the Golden Rule is, "Do unto others as you will have them do unto you." In business however, you need to go by the Platinum Rule, "Do unto others the way they want to be treated." There are many ways to approach business from an image standpoint but we tend to make mistakes that can be avoided very easily. The problem: we forget to pay attention to the details.

The following are some basic business image mistakes to avoid regarding the way you approach business:

- Sending out sloppy business materials
- Not doing what you say you are going to do
- Failing to say "thank you" in writing
- Not being punctual, nor informing of an absence
- Not answering important emails and voice mail messages in a timely manner

Of course these are very simple things but sometimes we get caught up in bad image habits. Just be aware and work on avoiding the common mistakes.

4. Your appearance. Looking great needn't be a big deal. It's a matter of having a simple routine. Here are some quick tips from my image consulting days:
- **Men**. Facial hair is not a business look, but if you choose to keep it make sure it fits the shape of your face and is trimmed regularly. Minimal cologne is best. Regarding jewelry, watches should be sophisticated and slender (no earrings or rings except for wedding bands). Always make sure your clothing is crisp and clean; most importantly that they fit. There's nothing worse than a man in suit and it doesn't fit correctly.
- **Women**. Keep jewelry simple and elegant; ensure your makeup is light and natural looking. Make sure nails are manicured, and use clear polish or a neutral color. Same goes for women when it comes to clothing as with men. In addition make sure to decide on your business look and stick with it order to project a consistent image. There are many ways to enhance a simple suit with color and accessories, just maintain the look and you'll be fine.

Special Note: Check your appearance in a three-panel mirror if possible. Watch for scuffs on shoes and wrinkles in clothing.

Guidelines for using color in dress
Color should not overpower you--it should complement your appearance. There are 3 ways to use color in business:
- Powerful - Use high contrast. *(Example: Black suit with white shirt)*
- Approachable- Use medium to low contrast. *(Example: Lavender top with dark purple pants)*
- Creative- Use patterns and different textures; experiment with dress. *(Example: A dark suit with a Bugs Bunny Tie)*

Do not allow your clothing to "wear" you. The wardrobe that works best for you and your business image is **less about fashion and more about *function*.**

5. Internationally Accepted Guidelines for Dress. Even if you do not deal in International business, you must know the internationally accepted guidelines for Business Dress. No matter where you are, if you see a sign with a fork and knife pictured, what does that mean? Food, right... That is what I mean by internationally accepted guidelines. Here are a few basic wardrobe pieces that works not matter your environment:
- **Men**. A dark suit, tie, and white or blue dress shirt.
- **Women**. Matching skirt suit, or a dress, or matching dress and jacket

These are a small portion of the things you can do to take stock in your image, but YOU are an important part in the achievement of your goals. **Having the correct outward appearance and the right attitude can, often times, take you farther than education or experience.**

Small Business Strategist, **Sherese Duncan** "the Entrepreneur's Strategic Partner," is President and CEO of Effició, Inc. the Business School for Entrepreneurs™. For more information about Duncan and her company, go to www.efficio.biz.

Strategies for Setting Up Solid Joint Ventures and Partnerships

By Anthony & Crystal Obey

"Together we can do amazing things." **Robin J. Elliott**

Without first learning how to approach potential Joint Venture partners, you will struggle to truly accomplish your goals and by reading this book, I'm sure you're starting to see the incredible value of working together with other people to reach your business and/or ministry goals!

You have to first understand that every potential partnership won't work out. Various reasons can be the cause of this including: your personalities don't mesh well, they're just too busy to think about anything else right now, you can't clearly see how you can work together, and so on. These are all just superficial things that don't really mean you will never work together, just not right now.

Though you can't control anyone and it's not practical to think that everybody should work with you even if it could really benefit them, there are some simple but critical keys to striking the maximum number of lucrative, win/win Joint Venture deals which include…

Key #1 Do Your Due Diligence - Do Your Homework

This is the first and single most important thing that you can do when seeking out new Joint Venture partners to work with. Even if you know the person very well, you want to spend adequate time preparing yourself, preparing your deal, planning your approach, and most importantly, getting to know what's in it for them. You need to do your homework on your potential JV partners to see how your relationship can be beneficial for all parties involved and to see if there's anything that would raise a red flag about the person you're learning about.

Google is a great asset to finding out good information about people. You can learn a lot by reading everything that comes up in the Google results. Nevertheless, not everything reported is always true or factual about people so you have to decipher and make a judgment on the majority of what you learn from a person.

Key #2 Plan the Perfect Approach

Nehemiah spent months seeking the Lord, studying and planning to make his great request of the king. Esther did her due diligence before entering the king's chambers. These two people provide excellent biblical examples of how critically important it is to do your due diligence before approaching people with potential deals. You need to write down your approach so that you can firmly, confidently, and seamlessly present your request, offer, or opportunity to people.

If you're emailing or mailing letters to people, you have to write a professional, well thought out letter that's friendly and softly gets people at least interested in returning your email. In a letter or email you don't have to reveal everything about the deal, and in most cases its best not to. You just want people to know that there's a potential win/win way you all can work together and you would like to schedule a few minutes of time to talk more if they're interested.

Key #3 Work With People You Know then Spread Out

This is the very first thing most MLM companies teach people to do. Some people feel embarrassed going to their family, friends, and associates asking them to join their team or try their product. But if you're too embarrassed to approach these people consider a few things. Is your offer or opportunity strong enough? Have you prepared a strong enough presentation which shows people what's in it for them and how they can benefit from it? Are they the right people to approach in the first place? Sufficiently answering these three questions could mean all the difference in getting laughable rejection and striking lucrative, solid Joint Ventures with people you know well.

Key #4 Discover Their Hot Buttons and Press Them Hard

When speaking or writing to the person(s) you're trying to partner with, you want to establish that you have something that they want and need and you would like to schedule a meeting or speaking over the phone about potentially working together. In this initial contact - email, mailing, phone call, or in person, you simply want to get the person interested by hitting their hot buttons. If you've got a way they can make some easy money, fast and you know they're feeling the crunch from the economy, let them know you've got a surefire way they can bring in some extra money simply using the skills, resources, or assets they already have. Once they say, "I'm interested," that's when you present your partnership idea in more depth.

Key #5 Memorandum of Understanding (MOU)

If you're concerned about it and if it's necessary, you don't have to sign a 50 page contract to make your agreements legal; a simple Memorandum of Understanding, using straight language that doesn't intimidate anybody is sufficient. You can let your lawyer look over this simple document and proceed with your exciting new JV. We have a free downloadable MOU at dollarmakersusa.com you can use and we've got a great way you can get top legal services for a mere fraction of what most people pay. The most important thing to remember here is to be very respectful of others and don't scare them away by throwing a contract in their face. You don't always need a MOU for every deal.

These are a few things that will get you off on the right foot to landing more Joint Venture partnership deals with less rejection, and building profitable long-term relationships.

What You Should Know about Branding Relative to Marketing

By Bob Ivory

"You know why Madison Avenue advertising has never done well in Harlem? We're the only ones who know what it means to be Brand X." -**Dick Gregory**

To understand branding you must first understand what marketing is. It may seem like a simplistic answer but it is true nonetheless; simply stated, marketing is everything you do to place your product or service in the hands of potential customers. Anything that you can imagine from packaging to pricing is a part of the marketing process.

So what is a brand? Let's first take the word and its literal meaning. For centuries iron symbols were crafted with the initials or emblem of the owner of property – often cattle and other livestock. The iron symbols were heated until red-hot then pressed against the hide of the beast. This was, and is, called *branding* which was done to identify ownership.

There is a lot of talk about what branding is. Some say your brand is what other people say about your product or service. I prefer to think of that as brand reinforcement. No one creates a product and says I'll let the public tell me what I have created. They may give it a nickname, but the identity of a thing comes from its creator. The word brand has come to mean "The Big Idea."

Some people confuse a logo with the brand. This is understandable since originally, for all intents and purposes the branding I spoke of earlier was done with a symbol, initials or letters. These are often the components that make up a logo.

However, brand, as we know it today is not a logo. A logo is the tangible identity of a company in the market. Logos can be emblems, signs or symbols designed to portray the image of a company. So you see a logo (which is essentially a piece of art) is not a brand. However, it is integral to the brand.

One of the best definitions I have heard that describes a brand was given at a seminar I was a part of a few years ago given by a colleague, Tina Polite. She said that a brand is a promise. I like it for its simplicity and its profundity. The image that represents the brand sends a message to you. The promise in the case of McDonald's is this: no matter where you go, under these golden arches you will find the burgers – and all that comes with them will always have the same consistent quality. It is an assurance of integrity.

A brand is about trust. It's about what people expect to experience when they come into contact with your brand. It's a perceived notion. It's what they count on when they buy into your program.

Instead of putting resources into a logo, how about creatively finding ways to communicate the message, mission and qualities of your business? Think fewer objects and graphics, and more conversations and experiences. Focus not so much on image – and more about reality.

Remember this: Excellence is unmistakable. The world of business is hugely competitive and is comprised of thousands of logos. Out of those thousands, only a few survive to become famous. There are certain factors that make a logo successful.

Here are some tips on developing a logo:
- It must be legible.
- The color combination should be suitable for the company.
- It must be unique.
- It should project the image of the company.
- The logo should not be complicated or cluttered.
- It Must be cost effective and as simple as possible.

- The logo should be effective regardless of size.
- It should not contain any complicated images or photography.

Branding is another word for integrated marketing and the logo is part of that overall marketing campaign that builds a brand.

Branding is all about saying the same thing and communicating the same key message, over and over again – until it's "branded" in someone's brain.

The key thing about a logo – it doesn't change. It can be repositioned or "updated" – but never changed. That would kill the equity you built in marketing the logo as part of your brand. When you create a new logo (or new tag line) you are starting over again.

It takes a long time build up substantial "brand equity" – don't destroy it because you have a new idea. Stick with your logo, tagline and other elements you have set in place. You want to get to the point with your brand so that it is embedded into the subconscious minds of your audience.

When it is in the psyche of consumers, they will automatically connect a phrase or photo with you. When you hear a name – you get a mental picture or think of a quality. If I say, TD Jakes or Oprah – you have an idea of what to expect from those "brand names." They are famous, true, but they are also a brand. And a brand translates in business into dollars. That's the bottom line.

A good example is Nike's "Just do it" campaign. That phrase and "swoosh" logo are their brand. Whether their shoes are better than others – well, that's how you see it. But regardless, you'll pay a premium price for their shoes because they've branded themselves that way.

Branding in business is about building an empire. What does your brand say about you? You can gage by checking sales figures. That is a good indication of how well your brand is doing.

I hope I have inspired you to step up your brand. In addition to gaining fame, recognition, stature and money – a good brand can make an impact and change lives. By having a good brand (or reputation), you can be a great influence in society. So take your brand seriously – it's part of your purpose. It is your God-given assignment to get it right.

Bob Ivory is a brand strategist, graphic designer, conference speaker and media consultant. He is a strategic partner of Ministry Marketing Solutions and Pam Perry. For more information visit www.ivorycoastmedia.com or contact Bob at bivory@ivorycoastmedia.com

How to Become a Magnet for Lucrative Opportunities & Great Partners

By Anthony & Crystal Obey

"Catch us the foxes, the little foxes that spoil the vines, for our vines have tender grapes."
Song of Solomon 2: 15

Quite simply, the single best way to becoming a magnet for the very best and most exclusive Joint Venture deals is to be an excellent person who produces excellent work. The very best people are always attracted to other high-quality people. Eagles recognize and appreciate other eagles. You will always get and attract what you project and produce. You get out what you put in. You've got to once and for all commit yourself to being a great person, a person of excellence, and a person who represents God well.

But the truth of the matter is that it really doesn't take a whole lot of extraordinary drive or talent to be considered a great person. Someone very successful said that the key to becoming more successful than 95% of the rest is to simply "Show up, show up on time, show up ready to work!" That was it! And when you think about it, you'll find that to be true. Most successful people aren't geniuses, and it may be true that most geniuses aren't successful. Being successful isn't a matter of raw talent and natural giftedness. Some of the world's worst terrorists and mass murderers were highly talented people but they had other 'issues.'

If you're technically a genius, great; but if not, don't worry; you can still bulldoze your way into the elite ranks of the top 5% of successful people by doing some pretty simple things. These are some of the things that you need to keep in mind when seeking to become the very best person you can be so that you can attract success and be an opportunity magnet.

Go After Something Bigger than Yourself

Look at how successful Moses and Martin Luther King Jr. were. They committed themselves to serving humanity and seeking some of the most basic human rights every man should have; freedom and equality. You can become a great person by committing yourself to serving an underserved people, bringing justice to an oppressed people, or offering better solutions to a stressed people. Wal-Mart is one of the top companies in the world because they serve some of the most basic needs of all people.

Never Stop Growing, Learning, & Innovating

You will beat 95% of the people around you just by consistently doing little things to improve yourself, your business, your message, and your ideals. *"It's been my observation that most people get ahead during the time that others waste time."* (Henry Ford) Most successful people, past and current, conclude that building massive, extraordinary success is done one simple task at a time. Henry Ford didn't say the smartest people, most attractive people, the funniest people, or the most talented people get ahead. No; he basically said that the tortoise always beats the hare just by being consistent. "Slow and steady wins the race."

Do a Good Job

Don't ever stop learning more about your business, industry, and market. Don't ever stop improving yourself and your work and you will eventually become the captain of your industry. I've seen people who had all the potential in the world, had a great position, and great opportunities to do something extraordinary fail to seize the moment because they didn't take pride in the work they did. In our business, we've done some of everything to get the job done. And what's amazing to me now is looking back at how we've grown to become more competent in some area simply because we wanted to do a good job and get good results. We learned how to do things simply out of necessity to sell our products and services. We eventually got so good at it that we were able to compete and get business offering these services to other people! We go after results and that is what we get.

Keep Your Word

The quickest way to lose a good partner is to show up late and fail to do what you say you will. We have zero time for folks who can't keep appointments and show common respect. You'll kill a good deal right off the bat by showing up late, making excuses, missing your deadlines, and not keeping your word. Keep all of your deadlines and do what you say you'll do.

Be Generous

When setting up your Joint Venture deals, pay your partners good commissions for helping you achieve your goals knowing that without their help you wouldn't have the business they're bringing you. So be generous when it comes to the actual business but also be generous and giving to them. Give people complements and more people will take an interest in you. Everyone likes to be complemented and everyone's favorite word is their own name. So relate to them, compliment them and you'll quickly make more friends than you can handle.

If you do these things, and most importantly, do them consistently, you will become a Joint Venture, partnership, and opportunity magnet.

Get Your Free Gifts Available at SynergyEnergyMarketing.com

What to Do Daily, Weekly, and Monthly to Brand Your Book

By Pam Perry

"The key is not to prioritize what's on your schedule, but to schedule your priorities." **Stephen Covey**

Most authors will not become millionaires unless they have multiple works or multiple streams of income that can keep their income level consistent. Otherwise, they will not be able to give up their "day jobs."

But there are ways to build momentum, expand your platform and solidify your brand so you are successful. Most authors tell me, "I don't have time" or "I don't know what to do next" or "I hit a brick wall – and I can't seem to get motivated to market anymore."

You can market yourself everyday just by doing these things. When I coach clients, these are the things I tell them to do on an ongoing basis:

Monthly
- Attend a writers meeting or critique group.
- Ask for reviews or endorsements from those you've given "comp" copies too.
- Attend a civic organization and tell the members what you do.
- Read trade publications like *Black Issue Book Review*, *Writer's Digest* or *The Writer*.
- Take a teleclass or attend another type of live internet event.
- Look for contests you can enter or awards you can nominate yourself for.
- Create a YouTube video message or be a guest on a local cable show.
- Hold or plan a teleseminar.
- Update your media list & research for new ones to add.
- Invite a media person you've admired to lunch.
- Participate at an event by speaking, presenting or teaching.
- Write articles and submit to article directories.
- Post reviews of other books you've read on Amazon.com.
- Write and post press releases.
- Write and pitch feature stories to the media.
- Create and distribute an online or direct mail newsletter.
- Reach out to bloggers and see if you can do a "blog tour" with them.
- Meet with your advisors, mentors or "master mind" partners.
- Add additional information to your website (i.e. a blog article, a link).
- Keep in touch with key bookstores that are selling your books.
- Email mini-courses to those who sign up via an Eblast that you send out.
- Manage back end tasks such as customer support, accounting, sales, etc…
- Look for easier ways to do business. Ask others what systems they use.

Weekly
- Give someone you meet one of your books and follow up in 30 days.
- Visit an online forum and participate or get some PR coaching.
- Look for new articles to read on internet marketing and joint ventures (Google).

- Listen to podcasts (look for the topic of interest online in a podcast directory).
- Send an eblast to your email list – giving them a tip or link to blog post you found helpful.
- Mail a handwritten note or postcard to someone you met in person or connected with online.
- Post to your blog & add a new feature to "amp" it up (get cues from other blogs).
- Drop postcards or bookmarks at places where you regularly go – bookstores, libraries, hair salons, cleaners, restaurants, Starbucks.
- Update your website by adding current "media hits" and interviews.
- Send an email to someone online you would like to connect with.
- Interact with a "group" on Facebook or LinkedIn.
- Get to know the key authors / leaders in your field. Follow their blogs or Google them to see what they are up to.
- Keep track of your stats on your website, blogs and Ezine opens.
- Do at least one blog talk show or at the very least call-in to one.
- Post a bulletin on your MySpace and add some new blogs.

Daily
- Write. Write. Write. That's your main job. Content is king!
- Read some trade pubs or read magazines in your niche.
- Comment on someone else's blog.
- Make a phone call to a media outlet you'd like to be featured on.
- Read the daily newspapers looking for topics you can comment on.
- Scan columns by the regular columnists and give feedback their blogs.
- Add friends to your Facebook, MySpace, LinkedIn accounts.
- Follow someone new on Twitter.
- Add people to your database that you meet or have not been in touch with (with permission).
- Add an automatic signature to all the emails your answer.
- Twitter by sending a link to your blog, or a favorite blog, or a free report they can download.
- Participate in message boards, chat group or yahoo groups that are industry related. (The Writers View is a good one – found on Yahoo and www.ChocolatePagesNetwork.com) This helps to increase exposure and give your information to stay on the cutting-edge.

For a creative writer and author, time is managed with calendars – not with clocks. What you are doing is leaving a virtual "footprint" everywhere you go – online and offline. These elements can be implemented with little or no outside help.

If implemented correctly and consistently, these mini-marketing tactics can help revolutionize your ministry or business in no time. By continually branding yourself with the key message of your platform, people will come to you for information and expertise.

Remember to have a marketing mindset and let people know why they should buy your book (mention the benefits of what the book will do for them.) Keep the main thing "the main thing" – focus on changing lives and making an impact for the Kingdom.

Building solid relationships is critical at every stage of branding. Don't expect instant results. Trust is the basis of all relationships. Trust is never freely given – trust is earned. Demonstrate your solid commitment and be willing to stay the course.

Where to Find All the Joint Venture Partners You Can Handle

By Anthony & Crystal Obey

"People are definitely a company's greatest asset. It doesn't make any difference whether the product is cars or cosmetics. A company is only as good as the people it keeps." **Mary Kay Ash**

It's an interesting progression. You start off trying to find a better way to market your business or add more streams of income so that your finances are more stable. Somehow, during your research you find out about the benefits of joint ventures. Then you decide that you want to be a joint venture broker part time or fulltime. You may just want to do them in your business, or you may be so intrigued that you want all of your income to come from joint ventures. Either way, at some point you are going to be faced with the big question of "OK, this is great, but how do I actually find Joint Venture Partners?"

Glad you asked because here are the best ways to have more partners than you can handle. Seriously, if you follow these instructions your problem will start out being the issue of finding partners and will turn into the issue of choosing only the best deals and managing the relationships.

This happens because once you get the hang of creating win/win deals you start seeing opportunity everywhere and every person you talk to could end up being a partner. And once you have one relationship in place the initial joint venture naturally spawns into more deals. When you stop trying to sell and start solving you'll find an abundance of people who have an endless list of things that need to be solved.

So take this advice seriously and do what you need to do so that you move from lack to abundance as quickly as possible.

Look at Your Current Relationships

Joint Ventures are all about relationships. You can set up deals with people who you don't know, and that is common, but it is easier to start by working with people you do know. All you have to do is link supply and demand and make sure you receive a payment. If someone you know needs or wants something, just help them get it.

Revisit Your Referral Relationships

Are you currently sending referrals to a businessperson but aren't getting any compensation? Most people are. You can't afford to continue building someone else's business. Talk to the people you are referring business to and let them know that you are changing your business referral system. Let them know that you are now paying a fee for any referrals and you would like to set up the same thing with them. If they say no then find someone else to send the business to who will compensate you. It doesn't have to be a monetary compensation but you do need something in exchange.

Join a Club for JV Brokers

Just like in any industry, there are clubs for joint venture brokers. You can find paid and free clubs. The number one thing to look for is if the club has members who you would like to partner with and if there is an abundant supply of opportunity for you to participate. With the club we are the USA Directors for, **DollarMakers**, members must abide by a code of ethics and bad members are fired. There is accountability and lots of opportunity to interact through technology and also in person. Plus it is worldwide so you can expand your business easily into other countries.

Change Your Networking Outlook

Stop going to networking meetings trying to sell your product. Those meetings have a room full of people looking for more business and have underutilized resources available. Start going to meetings with the attitude that you are there to help solve problems and you'll have lots of opportunity. As a joint venture broker you could get paid to link up people in that same room, or you can spend the hour trying to find out who is interested in your product. If you have been networking for a long time you have a lot of relationships that will never be fruitful for you unless you start thinking about win/win deals.

Join Your Competition

Traditional thinking says that you should hate the competition and pray that they fail. That is a mistake because there is unlimited opportunity available. You could partner with them and trade unconverted leads. You could send them business that you don't want to service and vice versa. You could combine services and create a new valuable offering for customers. That is how you eliminate your competition. Stop thinking in a scarcity way and start thinking in abundance.

If you do these things you will have unlimited opportunities. Just focus on doing your first joint venture and you'll build confidence. Then you will feel confident to set up another deal, and at that point you'll be well on your way to success.

Get Your Free Gifts Available at SynergyEnergyMarketing.com

Are You "Best Seller" Material?
Let's Test Your Marketing IQ. *Plus Ten Tips to Make "Best Seller" Status*

By Pam Perry

"It is for us to pray not for tasks equal to our powers, but for powers equal to our tasks, to go forward with a great desire forever beating at the door of our hearts as we travel toward our distant goal." **Helen Keller**

Test your Book Marketing IQ. Answer these questions:

1. What resources do you want access to?
2. What part of the publicity process seems to be the most difficult?
3. What would make your Book PR campaign a success to you?
4. What part of getting started is the most difficult?
5. Would you like media training for broadcast interviews?
6. Do you have a "30 second" pitch that you have memorized about your book?
7. Do you know how to speak in media-savvy sound bites?
8. Do you have a platform for your book – and/or have you built a demand or anticipation for your book?
9. Do you have a *professional* press kit and EPK?
10. Do you have a professional and up to date author photo? & good bio?
11. Do you know what goes in a press kit?
12. Do you have endorsements for your book?
13. Could your cover sell your book without YOU being there to explain it?
14. Do you have by-lines in other publications?
15. Do you have **The Christian Writers Market Guide** to know where to submit articles?
16. Have you employed a social networking strategy (i.e. Facebook, MySpace, Twitter) in your branding strategy?
17. Do you have internet ranking/presence? (Blog, Ning, website optimized?)
18. Do you sell books online? On Amazon?
19. Do you have your own media contacts? Do you know how to pitch to the media?
20. Is your book nationally distributed? Do you know how it's selling?
21. What writer's conferences do you attend or will you attend next year?
22. How often do you read marketing books and trade or writer's magazines?
23. Which books or magazines have helped you the most in promoting your book?
24. How often do you attend book signings of other authors?
25. Are you a member of a critique group, book club or writers group?
26. Do you have an ad budget? An advertising plan?
27. Do you know the top ten books in your genre and their websites? Do you follow their cues? Do you have a book mentor?
28. Do you join forums or yahoo groups and comment?
29. Do you subscribe to any blogs and post blog comments?
30. Have you ever been a "guest blogger" for any blogs?
31. Do you regularly send out press releases through the PR Wire services like Black Gospel Promo.com, ChristianPRGroup.com, PRWeb.com or BlackNews.com?
32. Do you regularly solicit testimonials about your book from readers?
33. Do you have postcards or book marks for your book? Do you put them everywhere!?

34. Do you have a book trailer?
35. Do you have a YouTube channel?
36. Do you podcast? Ever been on one?

Now, after you have done your self-assessment, here are the ingredients every best seller must have:

1. **Title** – is it gripping, interesting? Does it make sense? Would one know what it's about without reading anything else?
2. **Cover** – people do judge a book by its cover. Make sure it has enough punch to stand out on the shelves among the thousands of other books. Is it clean, neat and crisp – yet interesting?
3. **Endorsements** – what others say about you is key. Who these people are is even more important. Pull together the "best words from the best people." It will pre-sell your book before you even open your mouth. Continue to get reader reviews and testimonials even after the book is out. Add them to your blog or website. Put the endorsements on everything – not just the book. Put on postcards, business card (on the back). Put on Amazon.com.
4. **Writer's credentials** – do you have anything else with your byline? Do you blog? How well are you "branded?" Do you have an audience that actually likes what you write? Are you an expert in something? Advanced degree? Show it off. Now is not the time to be shy.
5. **Knowledge of the Market** the book will reach – and the author's reputation in that market. The author must create a market for himself by really addressing the needs of that market, knowing that market, understanding it thoroughly and communicating the right message to that market. Key to the success for any book.
6. **Timing** – in relation to other events going on in the world/society. Are there movies, songs or talk shows that are bringing up the subject you have discussed in your book? Do you read the newspaper regularly and respond with Opinion Editorials when they are discussing "your" platform/topic?
7. **Advertising** – targeting the right message to the right media at the right time. The ad does not have to be big, it just has to be consistent and an attractive ad.
8. **Media coverage** – publicity. The frosting on the cake. Getting on radio, TV and in newspapers and magazine and Ezines. Consistently (w/advertising too). You must have a "hook" and the timing of your pitches must be synchronized with what is going on in the world and what the reporters/producers are looking for.
9. **Distribution** – if you want to be a best-seller, you have to have your book available. Make sure you sign up with a distributor or wholesaler so it is accessible to bookstores. (Amazon is not national distribution…it is a website). Best-sellers are sold in real bookstores and they only order from distributors or wholesales. *(See Christian Writer's Market Guide for Distributors to approach. Note: You must have a press kit and solid marketing plan for them to consider you).*
10. **Word of Mouth** – the best advertising. This is what really sells books! The more "buzz" you have about your book, the better. How do you get people talking about your book? By engaging in their culture and creating messages in their media. Partner with other authors and find organizations to join your cause because of the synergy in messages. <u>Be relentless</u> in your goal to be a "best-seller" – and it will happen if you commit to the publicity process and pray for favor.

Get Your Free Gifts Available at SynergyEnergyMarketing.com

How To Get Started Partnering For Profit Fast!

By Anthony & Crystal Obey

"An enterprising person is one who comes across a pile of scrap metal and sees the making of a wonderful sculpture. An enterprising person is one who drives through an old decrepit part of town and sees a new housing development. An enterprising person is one who sees opportunity in all areas of life." **Jim Rohn**

If you want to get started finding partners and setting up joint ventures you need to do an audit of all your own resources and brainstorm about who would be potential partners. Once you start recording your resources and thinking about who you can connect with you will start to see how unlimited your opportunities are. After you fill in your audit form, the only thing you have left to do is start asking.

If someone doesn't accept your joint venture offer don't be discouraged. It just means that they don't understand or they don't see the value. If they don't understand then give them free books, articles, or audios on the benefits of joint ventures. If they don't see the value then find out what they need from you to make the deal work.

You may just need to negotiate a bit more, but many times you will strike a win/win deal. This is an exciting way to live and the more practice you get with identifying problems and finding solutions the easier it will become.

Use this form to get started and make more forms as you need to. This will help you solve some of your current problems now.

Instructions
1. In the first column list every need or want you have.
2. In the second column list who has what you want. You may know multiple sources so list them all so that you have options.
3. In the third column list what you have. List everything you have that someone else would find valuable for any reason.
4. In the fourth column list everyone who may want what you have.

Once the form is filled in you can think about how to approach your potential partner, put together your plan, then act on it.

What Do I Want?	Who Has What I Want?	What Do I Have?	Who Needs What I Have?

Get Your Free Gifts Available at SynergyEnergyMarketing.com

Book Promotion "To Do" List & Timeline

By Pam Perry

"The secret of all victory lies in the organization of the non-obvious." **Marcus Aurelius**

One year to six months before the book is out

1. Establish a board of directors and list of prayer partners
2. Build website & blog
3. Join and be active in your Writers Group
4. Look into attending ICRS or Book Expo
5. Create a marketing plan on how you plan to sell the books
6. Write book synopsis/description
7. Write fact information sheet/ compile media list for book galleys
8. Solicit endorsements for other authors, experts and "celebs"
9. Have professional PR photo taken
10. Secure a distributor/fulfillment plan
11. Collect samples of other authors' PR pieces or do online research
12. Take another author to coffee to pick their brain about PR ideas
13. Check on upcoming conferences, fairs, conventions for booth space
14. Begin your aggressive online strategy: MySpace, Facebook, Blog, Twitter, LinkedIn, etc.

Three months before the book is out

1. Compile media list for press releases (see rtir.com)
2. Compile direct mail list of friends, relatives, associates, etc.
3. Update author bio
4. Compile list to receive review books (get the Christian Writers Market Guide)
5. Design author/speaker/new book flier and/or brochure
6. Write press release & media alert
7. Decide about hiring a publicist or PR coach
8. Write and submit magazine articles
9. Send galley copies if your publishing house is not going to do it
10. Mail review copies to those you know can help get the job done
11. Network to create book signing opportunities
12. Find tie-in opportunities: homeschoolers, retirement communities, conventions
13. Work on news and feature write-ups for press
14. Establish relationships with other speakers for co-op selling (you sell their book and they sell yours at their back room table when they speak)
15. Compile endorsement page and quote review page post on website

Two months before the book is out

1. Write cover letter to send with galleys for book reviews
2. Plan launch party at book store or at a hotel/hall
3. Create Book Trailer and load up on YouTube
4. Secure speaking engagements

5. Design & print extra PR materials: postcards, bookmarks, T-shirts, pens, etc.
6. Contact local newspaper columnists and community newspapers / write columns

One month before the book is out
1. Send pre-publication announcements to media, friends, organizations
2. Schedule media interviews with local radio and TV stations
3. Write several professional talks based on your book
4. Develop key contacts with the influencers in your specialty field

3 weeks before the book is out
1. Get the word out that you're available to speak. Network.
2. Brand like crazy online and off line – network with others and get them excited about the book launch
3. Create an e-newsletter for your fan club and interested friends

2 weeks before the book is out
1. Call key contacts with the influencers in your specialty field & invite them to participate at your book signing/launch
2. Hire a photographer & psalmist for your event
3. Get an "award" ready for the person who has been most instrumental with you getting your book out (your mom)

1 week before the book is out
1. Confirm details of book launch
2. Personally invite media (again)
3. Make appointments for personal grooming (hair, nails, make up, wardrobe)

Continually
1. Pray a lot. Keep pushing on doors. Relentless promotion for a book is the key to success and sales.

This whole process can be overwhelming if you're not organized and don't have a team or some friends and other authors to support you.

Here is an Eight Point Plan to keep you on track:

1. **Write a press release.** Keep it short, to-the-point and informative. Give just enough information that would arouse the interest of the reader to want to find out more about the book. Send this press release out via e-blast services and new distribution services like BlackPR.com to hit magazines, newswires, radio stations, and TV stations across the nation.

2. **Create a media kit for the book.** This includes the press release, a great book cover, an awesome photo of the author, blurbs, book synopsis/description, endorsements, interview questions, a short bio of the author, the introduction, Table of Contents, copies of promotional materials and anything else necessary for the media kit (copies of previous clips, DVDs). Place all this in a personalized presentation folder. See www.vistaprint.com

3. **Get a professionally designed e-blast** through BlackGospelPromo.com and DetroitGospel.com to reach thousands in the African American Christian market via e-mail. This is a large part of the media blitz campaign because this e-blast will help to get the buzz going about your book and stirring up word-of-mouth. This has the potential to boost online sales because it hits the potential book buyer – and it's viral!

4. **Distribute and send out custom-designed postcards** to thousands of churches, bookstores, and libraries nation-wide. Postcards are a simple way for people to get an "idea" of what your book is about. Use postcards or bookmarks. Either one. See gotprint.com or vistaprint.com

5. **Advertise your book in newspapers and magazines** across the nation. Thousands of people, who will not otherwise know about your book, will run across it in the newspaper or magazine. Thus, more buzz about your book. See the Christian Writers Guide for suggestions.

6. **Do a podcast interview** on the Chocolate Pages show or some other blogtalkradio show. Then syndicate each interview across the internet and on various social networks. Great PR! (see www.blogtalkradio.com/ministrymarketingsolutions)

7. **Set your book up on numerous online retailer outlets** across the internet. Placing your book across the internet generates interest in your book from online users and gives these users the opportunity to buy your book now.

8. **Continually set up book signings** (or mini-seminars) and speaking engagements. Grow your database and continue to send out press releases and e-blasts when something new is happening in your campaign.

5 Quick and Easy Ways to Partner with Others to Reach Your Goals

By Anthony & Crystal Obey

"The way to get started is to quit talking and begin doing." **Walt Disney**

There are so many ways to partner with others, but sometimes it's hard to get the ideas flowing of exactly how to actually do it. We are providing you with 5 examples right here so that you can be inspired and come up with ways to accomplish your book, business, or ministry goals.

1. Time

If you don't have the time to do something don't just stop there. Find someone who has time and get them to do what you need done. In exchange you will want to give them what they want. Let's say you don't have the time to do extra filing in your office because your business has grown enough to where you need help but not enough help to hire an employee. Well, there are a lot of high school students who need experience for their college applications. They have time, and need office experience. You could offer to give them education in your field in exchange for their office help. This is a simple internship opportunity for them that will pay off how they need it to and it pays for you to have the extra help. You are helping them get the extra edge in their chosen field while at the same time getting your needs met.

2. Database

If you don't have a database please don't let that stop you. There is someone who has a database but needs something else. When you are trying to start a new business or ministry you will wonder how you'll reach the right people. If you have a women's ministry find businesses and organizations that target women. Then give them a free gift to pass out to their database as a gift. Give them a book, a consultation, or a sample. When they pass it out to their list, some of them will contact you to claim their gift. Now you are on your way to building your own list of people who have already shown interest in what you have to offer.

3. Equipment

You may run into a situation where you need to have access to another piece of equipment to start or grow your organization. The first thing you would naturally do is try to figure out how you can afford it. Instead of doing that, why not find out who already has the equipment? You could use their equipment when they aren't using it, and provide them with access to one of your resources. If you are an author and you need to use a camera to take photos for your marketing campaign, get someone to let you use their camera, or even take the pictures for you. Then give them what they need. You'll know what they are looking for by asking "What can I give you in exchange for using your camera, or for you to take my promotional photos?" Every person is different. You may have access to their favorite restaurant and can get them a gift card because your uncle owns the place. You may have lawn equipment that they need. You never know until you ask.

4. Skills

If you are trying to accomplish your goals but you run into the problem of needing a new skill, don't run out and get trained. Run out and find someone who has that skill! You might need to have a project done that requires graphic design work. Once you find a graphic artist who understands how to partner for success, you can get your project completed with excellence by a real professional and you can give them the exposure for possible referrals. That is cheap advertising for them. If they don't need advertising you could trade products, services, or any number of things.

5. Credit

If you are in a situation where you need a credit line to get supplies, you don't have to worry. Someone else already has credit there and you can work with them to get everything you need. If you own your own business and you need an office supply account you could partner up with someone who has an account. You could let them use part of your storage facility or whatever else they need in exchange for a certain dollar amount of open credit with the office supply store.

As you can see, there are many ways to get the job done. Don't ever let yourself be limited. Always ask yourself what you need and who has what you need. Then find a way to make the deal beneficial for you and your partner. Don't be discouraged if some people don't take you up on your offer. Just move on to the next person. There will always be someone who understands the power of partnering and who will jump at the offer to work with you.

Beyond the Book: Building A Platform

By Pam Perry

"This is no time for apathy or complacency, this is a time for vigorous and positive action. The great challenge you face is to be ready to enter these doors of opportunity."
Rev. Dr. Martin Luther King

So you were inspired to write and nudged to publish and now you are holding your dream in your hands: your book. It was a hard, tedious process – but you did it. It's so exhilarating.

Until you announce it to the world and everyone seems to yawn. Worse yet, no one is placing those bulk orders you'd hoped for or the phone is not ringing for you to come and speak and sign books.

Now is the perfect time for a little course in platform building by parlaying your knowledge and experience to become a recognized expert or "authority." After all, author and **author**ity are synergistic. You may not be famous or a brand name – but you can become one.

Here are some of the ways to develop a strategy that increases your brand equity, credibility and get you in the public eye:

1. **Know your stuff.** Don't be a fraud. If you're going to be an authority – study your craft. Devote time to developing your expertise by going to conferences, reading journals, newsletters and continuing your education.
2. **Join groups and network.** Don't just be a member – become involved. Volunteer to speak at industry events. Share your knowledge and information with others everywhere – high schools, career days, church programs, class reunions.
3. **Publish articles.** Write articles in those trade publications and write articles in local newspapers. Write letters to the editors in magazines and comment on stories relating to your platform. Though you have a book, you can repurpose a lot of that content in special reports, online blogs or in article directories like Ezine Articles. Think about publishing your own monthly Ezine too.
4. **Be a social media junkie.** Join Facebook, Twitter, Myspace, Linkedin and as many as you can handle. Load up the same photo, profile and key messages in each social network. Don't join if you are not going to be active though. That is bad branding. The more people see you – the more they will get to know you. Also by joining these social networks, your "google" ranking increases when people are looking on line.
5. **Enlist the support of noncompeting promotional partners.** Join a nonprofit group or a colleague in another part of the country and talk about doing seminars together or doing trade shows together. Share information, contacts and resources with each other and multiply each others voice to a particular audience. Promoting each other on your website or in your Ezine is a good way.
6. **Create an enormous email list and provide people with great content.** Do contests for your lists. Give away stuff. Keep them coming back and have them have you "top of mind." Plug your website and free Ezine in your email signature. Word of caution: don't be a spammer and avoid Email abuse by sending too many emails to your list. That's a quick way to lose a friend.
7. **When you set up a book signing (make it a mini seminar),** find a place to speak for free (school, church, professional organization) – send out a press release about it and garner some local media exposure. Contact the local newspapers, TV and radio stations and let them know

your local angle. With the broadcast media, tell them you'd love to come in and do an interview. With the print, offer to have them as your guest at the event or send them photos and releases after the event. (This is called post publicity).

8. **Develop a great website and add video and podcasts to it.** You can create your own video so easily today with a webcam or a flip camera – and load it up on YouTube. Instant "stardom." You don't have to be famous to have something to say on video. With YouTube millions are literally broadcasting themselves to fame. You can even count the amount of views your videos get.

9. **Make the most of your media hits.** When you are on the radio – ask for the interview and post it on your website. If you are featured in a magazine or newspaper – get the article, send it out to your email list and post it as a pdf on your website or blog. When you have a TV interview – that's right, post it up on Youtube and your website! Recycle the media by putting the information online in your social networks to.

10. **Make the media's job easy by being a great guest.** If you are a joy to work with, they will call you back and you can become a regular. How to be great guest – supply them with questions to ask you, talking points, be lively, be funny, be entertaining. And bring them an audience. Have the phone light up while you're on the air or have their website blow up or newsstands feel a hit because you're in their publication. That's a sure way to keep you on their radar.

11. **Give your promo pieces regularly to friends, colleagues and associates** – you never know how or when that postcard or brochure will garner you a major speaking engagement or interview. Keep handing out the material and reminding people about your expertise and how you love to share information.

12. **If a** national publication prints a story by or about you or your book, write a short news release about it for your daily and weekly newspapers, trade publications, Chamber of Commerce newsletter and alumni magazine. Media begets media. Think of it as snowball.

13. **Don't forget newspaper and magazine columnists,** who always need fresh ideas. Rather than asking them to write about you, invite them to one of your presentations. Or ask them to lunch. It's all about relationships. Make sure you follow their columns and blogs.

14. **After you've given a presentation or speech, offer to write a short article** summarizing your speech for the group's newsletter. Don't forget to offer your photo and ask them to post it on their website too.

15. **Join speaker's bureaus.** Get listed in BlackExperts.com and BlackSpeakers.com. These web sites are excellent directories to have your profiles listed on. Hundreds of journalists and meeting planners use these sites to find possible sources and speaking candidates. The cost to be listed is just $200 to $250 a year – but you can make 5 to 10 that from just one paid speaking engagement.

16. **Stay in contact.** Knowing the right people can be very helpful in branding yourself and getting speaking engagements and media interviews. Attend networking events and establish new contacts. From time to time, follow up with them – in person. Put them on your Ezine lists so that they know you still exist. Poke 'em on facebook.

How to Maximize Sales and Minimize Costs With Barter

By Anthony & Crystal Obey

"Everything we would ever need to become rich and powerful and sophisticated is within our reach. The major reason that so few take advantage of all that we have is simply, neglect." **Jim Rohn**

One of the least used secrets to dramatically cutting costs, increasing sales and maximizing your underutilized resources is the Joint Venture strategy called "Barter." This strategy can instantly take your business to a new level and help you live a far better lifestyle than you ever thought you could.

The definition of Barter is: to trade by exchange of commodities rather than by the use of money, to exchange in trade, as one commodity for another. You see, money is only used as a means of obtaining the goods and services we want. So a business takes your money and gives you the goods and services you're buying; and that money then allows them to obtain the goods and services they need. This makes up an economy.

Well there are networks called 'Barter Networks" that you can join that are, in essence, their own economy. In these barter networks, you can submit your goods and services for use in exchange of equal value of the goods and services you want to use.

Let's say you're a professional speaker and you charge $5,000 for one engagement. You can submit your services in a barter network and when someone books you at your normal $5,000 rate, you make $5,000 "barter dollars." This money is a credit valued at $5,000 that must be spent in your barter network. So let's say you're ready to take a seven day vacation to Jamaica. Your barter network sells resort tickets to Sandals (for example) and many other top resorts, but you settle on a Sandals vacation package in Jamaica for seven days. The hotel accommodations cost you $2,000 barter dollars so you have $3,000 barter dollars left. The only cash you pay is the barter network's small processing fee.

Get it? Why do you work? To make money, right? What do you do with the money? Buy the things that you need and want, right? So you're not just working for money, you're working for that trip, that new wardrobe, those beauty treatments, to eat at nice restaurants, for a new laptop, etc. All of these goods and services are traded in barter networks. So instead of using the money in your pocket to buy things, you can join a barter network and exchange some of the excess inventory you have in your business for that dream vacation you want to take!

Now then, most businesses don't operate at maximum capacity. Let's take a restaurant for example. How many restaurants have you been to the last month that didn't have all the seats filled? So their bills aren't decreasing just because those seats are empty but their profit margins sure are. You've probably never known a single restaurant to be filled to capacity seven days a week from open to close. That's underutilized space that lowers their profit margin. So a restaurant could join a barter network and sell gift cards to the other members and get more people in their restaurant.

By doing this, they'll make barter dollars that they can then use to buy the things that they want and need, like advertising or supplies. Plus, all those people who got the first meal free through barter, can become repeat customers and pay cash from now on and even bring friends! So marketing your goods and services in a barter network becomes a great way to market your business, increase sales, and plan on getting a lot of 'back-end' business from them and their friends who do business with you outside of the barter network.

Benefits of Barter

New Cash Sales – By starting off as a barter customer you can end up getting cash business from them and the people that they refer you to outside of the network. But in the meantime, you're earning barter dollars and taking exotic vacations, getting beauty treatments, and buying all the things you want and need inside the network.

Improves Cash Flow – Instead of spending your cash you can trade your underutilized resources and buy the things you want with barter dollars and do other stuff with your cash.

Moves Your Excess Inventory – If you own a clothing store and you want to get rid of some of your inventory in exchange for the things you're selling the clothes for in the first place, join a barter network and move those clothes…or whatever it is that you're offering.

Decreases Seasonality in Business and Downtime – You can increase sales and even out your business if it's seasonal by marketing through barter networks. By the way, you can join multiple barter networks.

Gives You a Competitive Edge – When people are trying to decide between two companies to use, they'll be more likely to work with you if you are both members of the same barter network. So offering a barter option opens your business up for more opportunities and puts you ahead of your competition.

Lowers Costs and Increases Profits – Selling your products and services through barter networks naturally lowers costs because you're not paying advertising costs to do it, you've already got the inventory anyway, so you might as well move it and get what you want in exchange. You keep more of your cash by saving up to 80% off of products and services.

Increases Your Buying Power – People who get good at 'working' barter networks live like kings without necessarily being rich. These people do have real assets and buying power, but it's just not recognized in the economy outside of the 'barter economy.' But they enjoy it in the real world!

Selling through barter networks is a very savvy way to do business. Some people do it exclusively and do very well, but it's just one of the many Joint Venture strategies that we teach people to use. It's a very powerful way to maximize your underutilized resources, market your business, bring in new customers, lower costs, increase profits…what more can I say? You should really learn more about this powerful way to live the lifestyle you want.

Bloggers and Blogging Can Create Publicity for Your Book

By Pam Perry

"There's a gold mine online." **Donna Baxter**

What's all the talk about Blogs? What's a blogosphere? Well, it's another vehicle to "get out there."

When I coach authors, I ask them if they have a blog. Then I ask them if they even subscribe to other blogs or even read and comment on other blogs. More times than not they answer, "No. Why?"

They are not trying to hear about blogs – they want to get on Oprah. They want front-page coverage and an appearance on a big show like "Good Morning America."

Well, let me let you in on a secret. The little guys with the blogs are now making some noise and blog tours are selling books. And, hey – if you're an author that's what you want, right?

Don't get me wrong, media coverage is great if you can get it. But not everybody who will want to know about your book reads newspapers, and circulation within the entire industry continues to erode year after year. As for that TV talk show, even if you get your 15 minutes of fame on "Oprah," the publicity is here today and gone tomorrow – unless you put in on Youtube. (Another PR secret).

We are in the era of what we call the "citizen journalist." Bloggers can "be the media" and are in a position to rapidly spread the word about your book. Google has changed the game for every body. Even media now look online for story ideas and to see what's hot.

So having a blog and getting mentioned in a blog will make you international – automatically by virtue of the internet. And your information will remain online for months and even years, waiting to be found by people who are searching for a book like yours.

Why blogs are so powerful for publicity

Here are the reasons why pitching to influential bloggers can bring you far more publicity than traditional media:

Bloggers usually write about niche topics. So, if you're writing a Christian novel or a book on church leadership, you can pitch it to bloggers who blog about Christian fiction and those who blog on Christian leadership. Targeting your message like a laser saves you a lot of time. Pitch only bloggers whose audiences would be interested in your book.

Unlike websites, blogs are updated frequently. Typically two to three times a week. The best bloggers – blog everyday. The more frequently you blog…the search engines will pick up your blogs and often give them a high position in google. This is called the organic search list.

Four out of ten journalists say they read blogs when looking for story ideas or researching their articles. In fact, many journalists are starting their own blogs. Here's a secret: If you want to reach a journalist quickly and make friends with them – don't send them an email – read their blogs and comment often. This will put you head and shoulders above all the other folks clamoring for their attention via email and voice mail.

Bloggers like to connect with other writers - unlike journalists who like to "get the scoop." So, bloggers frequently link to each others blog postings. So if one influential blogger writes about your product, other bloggers might link to it, thus creating viral publicity and hitting audiences you never knew existed.

Where to start your blog research

When you're ready to publicize your book, you can start researching bloggers by using google.com. Just type a topic and put "blog" behind it into the search box and hit "enter". It will return to you a list of blogs that include information about that topic. You can also go to Technorati.com and search there.

Once you've found a blog that looks like a good candidate for your pitch, spend some time reading it so you get a good feel for the type of things the blogger writes about and their style. Pay particular attention to whether the blogger refers to people who have emailed them to let them know about something. That's a good indication that the blogger is open to receiving a pitch.

One of the very best ways to get a blogger's attention before you pitch is to post a comment about a topic they discuss at their blog. I'll sometimes post two or three comments within a week or two at a particular blog before pitching that blogger with my idea. Why? Because I want the blogger to recognize me when I pitch.

I have a blog (www.MinistryMarketingSolutions.blogspot.com) and I pay close attention to everyone who posts comments there. It shows me they're willing to become involved in the conversation, not just contact me when they want something. This is good relationship building.

What not to say to bloggers

It's best not to pitch information about your book as part of a comment or it will look too self-serving. It's better to email the blogger, catch their attention and hope they write about you or your book.

Don't say things like "It would be nice if you mentioned this in your blog" or "Perhaps you might want to interview me for your blog." Just tell them about whatever you want them to know, and let them decide if they want to include it as a blog item. Unless you're doing a "special" blog tour.

How to Set up a Blog Tour

Now, you're ready to start contacting bloggers and you know how they blog and what they like. Contact them and tell them you'd like to do a blog tour with them and list all the other blogs you'd like to tour with. Says it's 10 to 14 bloggers during the week after Valentine's Day. Give them some time (about 2 or 3 weeks out) and see if they would be interested in blogging about your book during that particular week. They can interview you (called an online interview) or do a podcast (will talk about that later – but see www.blogtalkradio.com/ministrymarketingsolutions), or they can just post a review of some sort or write an article about the topic of your book and interview you for the story.

Always offer your book to them for FREE and even throw in some extra books for their blog readers just to sweeten the pot. Bloggers are people that you want to be friends with for a long time. They'll blog about you – and remember you'll want to blog about them too. It works both ways!

Make your PR stick – make it viral!

Now… visit My Blog and comment! http://www.ministrymarketingsolutions.blogspot.com

Get Your Free Gifts Available at SynergyEnergyMarketing.com

How Different Personality Types Affect Your Joint Ventures

By Anthony & Crystal Obey

"If there is any one secret of success, it lies in the ability to get the other person's point of view and see things from that person's angle as well as from your own." **Henry Ford**

Have you ever wondered why people act the way they do? Why some people can get things done so fast or so well while others can't even remember to do things, and some don't even want to do anything more than they have to? Have you noticed patterns in your life that make your actions and responses somewhat predictable to family and friends, or have you wondered how advertisers know exactly what to offer to you?

Well, that's a long answer but part of the reason is that there are basically four personality types and all people are unique and have parts of all the types, but there is one dominant type that natural rules them. Once you identify your dominant personality type and your secondary type you will be well on your way to learning how to interact with the people around you for maximum results.

You need to be aware of the different personality strengths, weaknesses, and motives. It will be easier for you to build rapport with people faster and it will make your interactions go more smoothly. There is no reason to cause extra friction simply because you didn't understand how to properly communicate. Also, during the course of your relationship you will know more of what to expect as you work together to accomplish the goal.

If you don't consider the differences in personality, you will find it harder to communicate with others, more difficult to find partners, and more stressful to achieve the results with each relationship.

To get you started with learning about the four types, here is a quick chart that compares the most popular titles. Just by quickly glancing at this chart you will start to realize that you and those around you really do fit into basic categories. This chart is just a start for you.

D.E.S.A.	Dominant	Expressive	Solid	Analytical
Hippocrates Greek Terms (370 BC)	Choleric	Sanguine	Phlegmatic	Melancholy
Biblical Characters	Paul	Peter	Abraham	Moses
Gary Smalley	Lion	Otter	Golden Retriever	Beaver
DISC	Dominance	Influence	Steadiness	Cautious Compliance
Children's Literature	Rabbit	Tigger	Pooh	Eeyore
Charlie Brown Characters	Lucy	Snoopy	Charlie Brown	Linus

After you have thought about the chart for a minute, make plans to do a quick test and find out what your type is. You can find a test at our website. After you see where you fit, start making it a habit to understand what type your potential and current partners are. Remember that your natural personality is a general tendency. A situation can cause you to react differently than your test results show and your motive can cause a huge difference too. So you want to use the personality testing as a tool to enhance your results but you don't want to look at people as just their test results. Every person is unique, has a mixture of all types, and is influenced by their past and current situation and environment.

To make your relationships stronger you will need to make some adjustments. Most conflicts happen when two opposite personalities collide. If you have a partner that is more aggressive, increase your aggressiveness so that you can run the race together and finish in record time. If you have a partner who needs more details, provide the information and the time they need to make a decision. If your partner needs more variety or more fun, make sure the relationship provides the social aspect they need. And if your partner needs to be motivated to make a decision give them a deadline and enough information to properly make a decision so that they can't keep you waiting forever.

As you learn more about the four personality types you will find it easier and more enjoyable to work with others and you'll seek out relationships that let you operate in your strengths while finding partners that fulfill your weaknesses.

Get Your Free Gifts Available at SynergyEnergyMarketing.com

The Power of PR

By Karen Taylor Bass

"If you set goals and go after them with all the determination you can muster, your gifts will take you places that will amaze you." **Les Brown**

When did public relations take over the world? Doesn't it seem that everyone is either PR savvy…or not savvy, at all? Is there no middle ground? There are professionals or celebrity "authorities" hawking products on every channel and many of us might wonder what they have that we don't. Well, the answer is, absolutely nothing.

As entrepreneurs, small business owners, and individuals with side–hustles, it is imperative that we understand the power of public relations and how to utilize strategic PR principles to be empowered *and* grow a successful enterprise. As a PR expert, I can admit that many of my clients didn't initially understand the power and value of public relations, but over time, we've begun to create new strategies, together.

In today's society, Public Relations can make-or-break a company. That said, there are 10 simple steps that I teach at my 'As Powerful As You Want To Be!' - PR Boot Camp, which can be put to use, right away, and take your company to the next level on a limited budget. Now, if you have an extra $3 – 5,000 to retain a publicist each month, you're on the fast track, but it never hurts to know how to do-it-yourself.

To move forward, it is essential to understand the difference between public relations and publicity – *public relations* is fostering public goodwill and creating a favorable opinion for a product, person or thing; *publicity* is simply the vehicle (i.e. TV, radio, magazine, newspaper, etc.), which brings attention *to* the product.

First, you must have a plan. You've got to be passionate, creative and strategic. Also, ask yourself a few questions. Where do you see your business – is it local, regional, national, global or virtual? What type of clients do you want to pursue and attract? Start believing in your hype, know that your story is unique and most important, talk yourself up to others like an A-List celebrity.

Here are 10 tips to implement as you create awareness and grow your business, right now:

1) **Define Your Mission.**
   What is your company about? What are your objectives? Who is your target audience?

2) **Be a Student of the Media.**
   Learn how the media works. For instance, be aware of who your desired outlet serves, what their deadlines are, when they publish or broadcast as well as their current trend for stories. Ask yourself what makes your story different. Not all media outlets are appropriate for every type of business.

3) **Be Prepared for the Opportunity.**
   Create a media kit, which consists of a press release announcing your company/product to seduce the media and entice clients to patronize your business, a biography (your life story, 1-2 pages with interesting information), a headshot for the media to run your photo and of course, a professional business card and website.

4) **Think Linearly.**

Act with a *plan*. Identify what you want to promote, the audience you want to reach, the tools you'll need (press release, etc), and media vehicles through which to accomplish your goal.

5) **Promote yourself.**
Brand *you*. Remember, you are an authority in your field, so begin to visualize, and execute your plan via public speaking engagements at schools, colleges, organizations, etc. Write an editorial or op-ed column, blog, appearance as a guest on local TV, public access, and/or talk radio. Network and work your magic every time.

6) **Polish your image (outward *and* inward).**
Are you sending out the message that you want? If so, what is that perception? Ask your friends and family members what impression they have of you.

7) **Secure a Committed Mentor.**
Make certain that the mentor you choose has time to *be* a mentor. Be clear with expectations and time and make it a two-way street. What do you have to offer? Also, be sure to give back to someone else who might be in need a mentor.

8) **Create and Maintain Key Relationships.**
Identify folks with common interests *and* different skills. Be a good friend and stand by your word.

9) **Empower Your Life.**
Give back. A great deal of business is done while volunteering, which can provide you a legitimate aura of leadership, dedication and commitment. Expand your base of key contacts. Become a board member and create a positive perception of who you are.

10) **Honor Your Process, Believe Your Hype.**
Remember, you are the best person for the job and you are *entitled* to success. PR is about knowing your worth and not underselling yourself to secure and/or maintain business.

The time to position yourself for an opportunity is *now*. Editors, TV bookers, publishers, online outlets are looking for original, inspiring and creative stories to capture each hour, day, week and month. Get started and be your own publicist.

Karen Taylor Bass, *owner of Taylor Made Media LLC and strategic partner to Pam Perry of Ministry Marketing Solutions Inc., is a PR Expert and coach located in New York. Visit her at www.taylormademediapr.com and www.theprdistinction.blogspot.com too.*

Maximum Output – Minimum Time

By Anthony & Crystal Obey

"If you have run with the footmen, and they have wearied you, then how can you contend with horses? And if in the land of peace, in which you trusted, they wearied you, then how will you do in the floodplain of the Jordan?"
Jeremiah 12: 5 NKJV

Why is it that everybody in the world seems to be running ragged all the time? Everybody's busy, busy, busy, just like a swarm of bees that get frazzled when there's an invader to their hive. Been busy doing the urgent and unimportant doesn't make us important. And being 'soooo busy' is not a badge of honor, but an embarrassment.

You see, it should be embarrassing to say that you're 'sooo busy' when you're telling that to someone who has 10 times the responsibility that you do and produces 10 times more than you do. It's a poor excuse to tell a successful business person you're hoping to strike a deal with that you showed up late to your appointment with them because you were doing this or that; you were busy. So how many important responsibilities do you think he/she has on their plate and they still made it to the appointment on time? What you're really saying is that you can't even manage the little responsibility that you have now, so you're definitely not ready for any real success!

Stop making the excuse that you're too busy to do the things you need to because anybody with good sense is going to hear something completely different than what you say. So you say one thing and they hear the real message; for instance, "I wish I could workout & eat right but I'm too busy…so I'll probably die early," "I wish my spouse and I could spend more time together but I'm too busy…so I'll probably lose the love of my life," "I wish I could start my dream business like you but I'm too busy working this dead-end job that I hate!"

If you want to have more time, get more done, and finally take control of your life, here's some tips we use to get it done.

Tip #1 Set Your Priorities

The priorities that you set will determine the very course of your life. Whatever is your top priority will determine who you become and what you get out of life. Having the wrong priorities can land you squarely into disaster. So seek God about them, search your heart, think about where you ultimately want to be 10 years from today and who you want to be.

You should pull out a notebook and pen and make a list of all the key areas to a successful and fulfilling life, right now. This list should include several key areas such as a. God b. Marriage & Family c. Heatlh, Wellness, and Fitness d. Personal Finances e. Business/Ministry f. Hobbies g. Life & Home Maintenance h. Friends etc.

Next, you should decide how much time per week and month you want to invest into each of these areas based on your goals for each of these areas. Then you can create a solid daily schedule from this list of priorities by allotting so much time to devote to managing each of these priorities. By doing this and following your new schedule every day, you can literally conquer anything, achieve anything, build anything, and become a master at anything you want! We produce a lot and get a lot of things done in a day as we build businesses, financial assets, and various streams of income, and yet we're building our relationship with God every day, building healthy and strong bodies every day, and building a healthy and fulfilling marriage every day. We do this by allotting some time to each of our priorities so that everything important to us gets some time. We water all the fruits of life we want to grow.

Tip #2 Always Keep Maximum Control of Your Time

Whenever we feel like we're getting too busy we have to determine the best course of action to re-gaining our peace and the control of our lives. We may just be in an extra busy time that we just have to muscle through with an end in sight, or we may have to decide to cut out some things and re-organize our priorities so that we get back to our peace. Jesus said, "Come to Me; My yoke is easy and My burden is light." God has taught us the critical message of learning to "Abide in Christ" and we find that the success of eating an elephant comes much easier by consistently and diligently taking one manageable bite at a time. If you're feeling too overloaded with responsibilities then you must come back to your top priorities and decide what needs to be cut.

Tip #3 Beware of Time Leeches

If you're volunteering in five ministries, serving on eight boards, and watching other peoples' kids all the time while your own husband is at home begging you for more 'quality time' or your own children are getting poor grades in class while you're 'watching the game every night' then you need to check yourself. Get your mind right and your priorities straight! God's not giving you any brownie points for sacrificing personal time with Him and quality time with your spouse and children, so you can run the church; not even if you're the pastor! And you definitely shouldn't sacrifice your important relationships for your business endeavors, so write time slots for everything in your daily schedule, including 'quality-time.'

Tip #4 Use Other Peoples' Time

As you build your business you need to really begin to learn how to effectively outsource and delegate authority and responsibilities to others. Jethro helped his son in law, Moses, learn the valuable lesson of delegation and team building. If you can afford a maid, hire one. If you can, get a virtual assistant. First, get one, then two, then ten. And finally, learn how to build your business in the most leveraged and automated way as possible, meaning that you're employing the work of others while maintaining maximum profit. It's being done by many business people every day. Read "The Four Hour Workweek."

If you plan on running with the 'big-boys' and doing 'big things' then you can't let your lack of time management defeat you. We've all got 24 hours in a day. Get more information on effective time management to master your time so you can get more done.

Get Your Free Gifts Available at SynergyEnergyMarketing.com

How to Hire and Work with Your Publicist or PR Coach

By Pam Perry

"The two most important requirements for major success are: first, being in the right place at the right time, and second, doing something about it." **Ray Kroc**

So you don't know anything about PR and you hope the people you hire know their stuff. But how do you even find, interview, hire and work with this key link in your media campaign?

What does a publicist or PR coach do?:

- Prepares or evaluates promotional material such as press kits, press releases and enticing emails
- Submits news releases and E-Blasts to media outlets or gives you the services to use
- Schedules radio and/or TV interviews; or shows you how to deliver a snappy phone pitch in 15 to 30 seconds
- Schedules local and national appearances and/or book signings or provides you with people to call
- Has a plethora of resources, contacts, and connections in the industry & they invest time in developing and nurturing strong relationships with their media contacts
- Gives you creative ways to market your book (keeping your market in mind) and knows exactly what you need to accomplish a publicity campaign

Guidelines for Picking a Publicist or PR coach:

- When meeting with a prospective publicist/PR coach, casually ask for the names of three clients who could recommend her services. If she feels good about the work she's done, she will quickly and enthusiastically come up with several names on the spot. Or just look on their website and contact the clients directly yourself.
- When you have the reference on the phone, ask him to name the best thing the publicist has done for his company. Ask specifically about results.
- Ask the publicist what she does best. Her answer should be something you think you need. If she specializes in something you don't need, she may not be right for you. (One point of caution: be open to new ideas!)
- Ask yourself, "Is this person as smart as I am?" A good business person always strives to surround himself with geniuses! At least, you will want to hire someone who seems very bright.
- Don't just ask the publicist what she costs—ask her *why* she costs what she costs (and do a comparison to other firms).
- Take note of whether or not she asks intelligent, thoughtful questions about your company. You don't want a publicist who makes a lot of (wrong) assumptions!
- Define up front what a successful marketing plan looks like, and determine a schedule for deliverables. It is imperative that both parties begin the relationship with the same expectations.
- Don't be stiffed by your publicist's vendors or settle for poor quality. Ask her how she chooses vendors, who her vendors are, and why. Leave vendor options open; three bids is not unusual. Does the vendor's portfolio of work wow you? Even one "dud" should disqualify them, because if they are capable of doing bad work, they will do it for you.
- Be sure she is a team player, not a superstar.

Now that you've picked a publicist, here are some Do's and Don'ts:

Do's

- Tell them your schedule & where you're speaking and what events you are planning
- Give them ample time to process your requests and return your phone calls.
- Tell them things that come across your desk or emails that would help them get the word out for you. They can't be everywhere all the time – sending FYI emails or Faxes are fine.
- Tell them if you get a good response from an interview.
- Tell them your "wish" list of media interviews and hosts you'd like to talk to and WHY.
- Give them as much background on you as possible: schools, awards, speaking engagements, places of employment (any place where there have been gatherings of people that know you or about you).
- Help other author friends. You reap what you sow. Look out for others.
- Keep an up-to-date database. Everywhere you go and speak – add to your mailing list. Emails especially!
- Send personal thank you notes to the media. Keep in touch with them – but don't be annoying.
- Give them ideas. Discuss new publicity angles. Publicists work with a variety of clients and they appreciate clients that are engaged in their publicity process and can see natural opportunities that they might miss.
- Give them good materials to work with: a great book cover, a good head shot, a great book title and great endorsements. Have a good business card too (with photo if possible).
- Be nice to the media and get rid of the "entitlement" attitude.
- Whenever possible, advertise on the media stations/TV or in the media outlets you're featured in, especially if you get a good response.
- Remember to say your book title and website several times during the interview.
- Follow the advice, suggestions and recommendations of your publicist.
- Let your publicist know your expectations right from the beginning.
- Be grateful to your publicist and show appreciation for their efforts. Tell them.
- Be consistent with the media.
- Make a positive confession about your publicity campaign and ask for prayer from your "inner circle," including your publicist. They're your "cheerleader" and intercessor.
- Research & know your market and ask them what "buzz" they have heard about your book and what you could do to improve.
- Critique your interviews and constantly improve your "sound bites."

Don't

- Reschedule an interview directly with the producer or reporter. Go through the publicist.
- Ignore interview requests.
- Take credit for your "media" success – know that it's God that orchestrates everything and a team that helps you LOOK good.
- If you have a question about the interview, ask your publicist immediately. Don't ask the interviewer. They'll take it as a bad sign that you don't know your facts or what you're doing.
- Don't lie or over exaggerate the truth to the media. They check you out anyway.
- Call your publicist after work hours or on the weekends unless it's an emergency – they're human too. The have their own lives, although they love you and your book, give them some space.

- Complain to your publicist if they can't get the media hit you're looking for right away. It may come in time, but it may not come at all if you're negative. Faith and patience produce the promise.
- Expect your publicist to know everything and everybody. Give them updates and FYI's via email. Keep in contact but don't be a nuisance.
- Assume that the media will give you copies of the story or the interview. Ask before the interview begins, or better yet, tape them yourself and/or subscribe to their periodical/newspaper via the website.
- Be a lone ranger. Connect with other writers/authors/speakers. Go to other author's book signings. You reap what you sow.
- Be antagonistic with your publicist – they can be your best friend or worst enemy. Do unto others as you would have them do unto you.
- Think you're a failure if you don't get on Oprah.

How to Work From Home and Not Be Alone

By Anthony & Crystal Obey

"A friendship founded on business is a good deal better than a business founded on friendship." **John D. Rockefeller**

When you first start working from home you are excited about the one minute commute and the fact that you don't have to sit in traffic to get to work anymore. You like having the option to raid the refrigerator when you want to and of course not having to dress up to head into the office. The benefits are endless and the freedom is exhilarating.

Depending on your personality type exactly how long it takes, sooner or later the loneliness of being away from coworkers sets in. You start to remember how fun it was to discuss the latest national news story or epidemic. You miss the office holiday celebrations, and maybe even the office drama. Your coworkers had become a family, though a little dysfunctional, but a sort of family to you. And depending on how long you worked at the same place, you built relationships that carried you through many life changes.

Now, you are working at home, running your own schedule, but silently suffering from people withdrawals. Maybe feeling a little bit on the outside now because most people get up and actually go somewhere to work and you are in a new club now, and your family and friends don't understand it at all.

Well, the good news is that you can have all the benefits of working from home and still enjoy a healthy dose of human interaction. You can work from home to be highly productive and incorporate a few tricks of the trade to keep your work life fulfilling with outside relationships.

The first and most obvious step is to join a professional organization. You'll have local and virtual meetings so when you want to get out and talk to people you have that option, and you can use the virtual tools when you aren't feeling so social. Make sure to join a group that puts you in contact with the type of people you want to do business with so that you aren't just wasting time. It's not wise to fill your schedule haphazardly with a bunch of meetings, but a few key memberships could be just what you need to stay in touch with potential clients and colleagues.

The second step is to join a support group where you can learn more about your direct industry. This way you can continue learning and growing with others who are in the same boat as you. The camaraderie will encourage you when you want to quit and seeing the success of others will inspire you to grow. You should attend the regular meetings and annual events so that you feel like you are part of a group trying to achieve the same goal and by doing this you'll see personal and business growth while at the same time meeting great people.

The third step is to take your work someplace else. Most people who work from home could easily do paperwork, research, or other activities that don't require more than a laptop or phone someplace else. What's stopping you from going to the bookstore, library, coffee shop, or park to work once a week? By being in a new environment you could be inspired with creative ideas for your business. You could also meet some interesting people who could end up becoming clients or partners.

The fourth step stays on the same line as working someplace else. You should make it a habit of scheduling all of your in-person meetings somewhere that you enjoy going. If you want to have a lunch meeting, do so, but not too often. Meals cause meetings to be extended, but getting out of your house can help you feel less isolated. Meeting in person instead of over the phone can help build your relationships so it is good to do to the extent that it is productive.

The fifth step is to work with people you like. You may be under the false impression that you have to work with anyone who is willing to work with you. That is absolutely not true. If you have customers who cause headaches, stop selling to them. If you have suppliers that cause you trouble, get new suppliers, and if you have partners who are more trouble than they are worth, by all means, get rid of them! Just by improving the satisfaction of the current relationships you have your life will be more pleasant.

Imagine being able to work with people who you like so that it is a pleasure to call them. It's like talking to old friends when you call your vendors, and your customers are worth serving. It can be like this for you and as long as everyone does their part your working relationships will be an asset for your work-at-home situation.

Basically, by putting a little thought into it you will see that even though you work from home you aren't alone. You are in a unique position to build deep long lasting relationships that provide more enjoyment for your work life. You are in control so when you need more interactive with others you can get it and when you need to be alone you can make that happen too.

How to Write a Press Release and Have it Do What It's Supposed to Do: Generate Some Buzz

By Pam Perry

"Always be magical, for that is what you truly are." **Natasha Munson**

This may come as a shock but just because you've published a book doesn't mean that it's worthy of some ink or air time. As a matter of fact, with over 200,000 new books a year – it's pretty regular. Getting media to pay attention to a release about a new book is not as easy to do any more – even if you have a great cover, title, endorsement and a flawless press release.

But you still need a press release (sometimes called media release, sometimes called news release) – regardless of what kind of media attention you're looking to garner. The release is the corner stone of the press kit and the primary vehicle to communicate with the media. It shows that you know the industry and you're not an amateur (unless it's not in the right format and badly written). If that happens, you will be labeled as someone who is too "green" and new to be worthy of news anyway.

The basic rules are clear: useful, accurate and interesting information portrayed within the set journalistic guidelines.

So, what goes into a press release? How do you make sure to make it to first base with the media?

Here's a checklist:
- Company Letterhead, Name, Address, Phone Number, email, Web Address
- PRESS RELEASE in all caps
- Contact Person's Name
- Immediate Release or Release Date (all caps)
- HEADLINE or TITLE in BOLD/CAPS
- BODY-Date/City-who,what,when,where and why
- Catchy Text
- Sum it up…
- Basic Font, Page Numbers, and ###
- Action Plan/Calendar

How should the press release be written?
- Give it a short meaningful title
- Make sure it has a "hook" and some real news
- Speak to target audience and be relevant (not too churchy)
- Don't pad it with fluff – don't go overboard with superlatives
- Emphasize benefits (to the audience) not features of your book
- Use powerful words that evoke interest and propel people to be ready to buy your book
- The shorter the press release – the more likely it will be read (one page is best)
- Make it idiot proof (meaning – put all the key info in it. Editors hate tracking down details like book price, ISBN, publisher, etc.)

The "meat" of the press release is pretty much to "why should anyone care?" copy. Press releases and news stories are boring to journalists without a 'human interest'. So here is your template:
- The body of the press release is very basic; who, what, where, when and why.

- The first paragraph of the press release should contain in brief detail what the press release is about.
- The second paragraph explains in detail: who cares; why you should care; where one can find it; when it will happen and who endorses the book
- The third paragraph will also include the second 'informative' paragraph and is **generally a quote** that gives the release a personal touch.

- The fourth and generally final paragraph is a summation of the release and further information on your company with the company contact information clearly spelled out.

From my 20 plus years in the PR biz, I've found that these are the main reasons why press releases are not picked up:

1. You wrote an ad; not a release. It's not a news release at all because all it does is sell. There is no solid news, valuable information, education, or entertainment.

2. You wrote it too "churchy" and alienate other people in the audience. Other news releases that are clearly written for the majority of this audience will win out over yours.

3. You are the center of attention in the release and you're not even famous! You focus on your books and your marketing, instead of on things that the editors and their audiences will be interested in.

4. You forgot to put the five W's up front—Who, What, Where, When, and Why this audience will be interested in this material.

5. You are too wordy and have no "HOOK." You focused on details and minutiae instead of on the most important ideas, issues, factors, facts, and news angles.

6. You included logos and other graphics that distract the editor from your key message. You may have also used a too fancy font or a file format that does not transmit over the web to everyone the same way.

7. You supplied a personally biased article instead of pitching your idea in terms of objective reasons in which the media audience will be interested. Save the personal articles for Op/Ed (Opinion editorials).

8. You wrote about features and facts and forgot to explain what they mean to real people. Tell a story with human interest. Give a reason to "why should I care."

9. You tried to be clever or cute - but you came off naïve, less than expert, flippant, arrogant, or crazy. Tone it down. Be normal. Play it straight.

10. You provided poor contact information. Identify the best single point of contact so that interested media people can reach you and get the attention and response from you that will meet their needs. Your release should list one key person (not the author), one phone, one e-mail address, and one URL (with no long string addresses).

11. You sent the release to the wrong media and you relied on an e-mail to produce an avalanche of media calls. You conducted no follow-up. How crazy is that? Follow up properly and you can triple

or quadruple your media response rate. Never ask, "Did you get my release?" Just ask, "What can I give you to support a feature story and meet your needs?"

The loved and loathed "release"- it can be a friend to the media or if not well-written or pitched the right way can be a foe. Take the time to research the media contact before shooting out into the universe. If you're using a press release distribution service (i.e. BlackPR.com or ChristianGroupPR.com or PRweb.com) make the release appeal to the end consumer because it may show up in blogs or be read directly by the target audience via a google search – which happens a lot

The next time you write a news release, please review it against these criteria to see if you've made any of these errors. Then fix each and every one of them. If you pay attention to these issues, you should have some success.

How to Make Your Marriage Partnership Work

By Anthony & Crystal Obey

"I believe that being successful means having a balance of success stories across the many areas of your life. You can't truly be considered successful in your business life if your home life is in shambles."
Zig Ziglar

According to the National Federation of Independent Business, one in five small businesses is run by a husband and wife team. That means that 20% of businesses are established by partners who live in the same home and are partners in life, love, and business. This adds extra responsibility and poses extra risks. It also holds the potential of extreme excellence and fulfillment.

If you believe that partnering with others is a great strategy then you will at some point wonder whether partnering with your spouse is a great idea. If you are considering it or currently have a husband and wife business arrangement then you want to make sure to follow a few guidelines so that your marital bliss doesn't become a big mistake and your business dreams don't become big disappointments!

Be Nice

If you are working with your spouse you will be tempted to let your emotions rule and not be as careful about your words and actions. In order to keep your relationship in tact you need to treat your spouse with the same courtesy and respect that you would a boss or employee. Don't yell, don't say mean things and don't be disrespectful. Use your manners and create an atmosphere of peace rather than tension. Don't take things too personally and especially don't bring business issues into the marriage, and marriage issues into the business. Keep things in their place and you'll enjoy your marriage and your business more.

Know Yourself

One of the worst things you can do is take on responsibilities that you can't handle. It is not good for your self esteem and it's not good for the team. You need to take the time to get to know your strengths, your weaknesses, your likes, and your dislikes. Once you know yourself well, you can handle the things that you do best so that you add the most value possible to the business. Simply delegate anything that you can't or don't want to do to employees, outsource it to vendors, or eliminate it from your business. The better you feel about yourself the better you will treat your spouse, and the better your business and marriage will be.

Know Your Spouse

Just like you need to take the time to know yourself, you need to get to really know your spouse. If you know their likes, dislikes, strengths, and weaknesses, then your expectations about what they bring to the partnership will be more realistic. You'll know what they can handle and can't handle so you can divide up the responsibilities appropriately. Since you are usually married to someone who is completely different than you, you'll have double the human resources to get the job done. Just don't let your expectations be based on other people or other businesses. You and your spouse are unique and your business needs to reflect the best of the both of you, together.

Build Your Marriage

Just because you work together and spend lots of time together doesn't mean that your marriage will be trouble free. Your marriage is completely separate from your business and it needs proper feeding and care on its own. You should have date nights where you don't talk about business and learn marriage building techniques and strategies with the same vigor that you put into your business.

The last thing you want to do is put all of your energy into your business together, then suffer a big business setback and be left with no business and no marriage. Build your marriage, and build your business separately. You are playing multiple roles and you need to treat them that way. Your spouse may need for you to support them as a spouse. Your business partner may need you to motivate them to get the job done. You need to know which role to play at what time. And yes, you are a spouse first, then a business partner, just in case you were wondering.

Feed Your Interests

When you work with your spouse you may find that the business consumes all of your conversations. To keep that from happening and to keep the spice in your marriage you need to feed your own interest. That means you need to have more going on than the business. In the start up phase of a business you can be super busy but you need to always remember that having something else to talk about is not a distraction from your business but it is an investment. It will keep you from getting burnt out. Enjoy your hobby as much as possible, read great books, and nurture relationships with family and friends. This will keep you from despising your business or growing bored with your spouse.

Be Clear On the Vision

You need to write the vision and make it plain. Discuss your goals for your business, establish roles, and keep communication lines open. You are on the same team and as long as you are both heading in the same direction your partnership will create exponential results. If you are divided you won't be successful. Revisit your vision often and make adjustments as needed, but the main thing is to stay in unity.

If you follow these guidelines your marriage partnership will be a blessing and not a curse for you and everyone you serve together.

What are Public Relations Retainers, PR Coaching, & Pay-Per-Placement Programs?

By Pam Perry

"Never be concerned about the price until you know the value."
Pam Perry

I am always surprised by what people think public relations services cost. When I ask them what their goals are, they'll say "to sell 10,000 copies." When I ask, "what's your budget?" they'll say they "I really don't have one – but maybe $500 to $1,000."

For a campaign that sells 10,000? I don't think so. If you could publish a book and spend $500 and sell 10,000 copies – you're a miracle worker. The fact is that you have to invest in your marketing (advertising AND public relations).

The Coaching Model

Now, as a PR coach, I help people save money by showing them how to do it themselves. I lay out a strategy for them, critique their timeline and plans – and give them the resources and contacts to make it happen.

Things I do for clients as their coach:
- Evaluate and improve their book marketing plan, tweak their ideas and give them new ones
- Tailor their promotion plans, tapping into my wealth of PR strategies and secrets
- Provide them with a full rolodex of the media and publishing contacts that make the difference
- Hold them accountable as we work together on their execution of the plan

It's really quite simple – if they invest the time and put forth the effort to really do what is required they'll reach their publishing goals. Coaching programs are typically $500 to $1,000.

I freely share my publicity strategies and contacts with authors, so everyone can have access to PR best practices - both basic and advanced - so they can market their messages to the masses.

The Retainer Way

Then there are those who want to hire a publicist to do the entire publicity campaign for them – from writing the marketing materials and distributing press releases to pitching media and scheduling interviews. This type of client is usually a publisher who has a "brand" name author and a projected print run of 20,000 or so books. The cost of a typical PR campaign like that will range from $5,000 to $7,500 for three months – with no guarantees.

Here's what they can expect from these types of campaigns:
- A fully developed press kit - interview questions, bio, endorsements, previous press clips, press release(s) and pitch letter(s)
- Reviews in the trade publications like *Publishers Weekly, Christian Retailing* and *Black Issue Book Review*
- Mailings to major media seeking TV interviews with TBN or Daystar and articles in *Upscale* or *Ebony*
- Radio interviews (In some cases a publicist will arrange a Radio Tour - several radio interviews in one day)
- Scheduling/Coordination of Book Tours and Media Appearances

- Online presence – email campaign blasts to targeted audiences, podcasts and blog tours
- Continuous mailings to media that request interviews and coverage (which is typical for a 'branded' author)

Pay-For-Performance or Pay-Per-Placement

Another approach that's getting an increasing amount of attention is pay-per-placement PR – which I have done for certain types of clients (usually after coaching). However, the pay-per-placement approach isn't for everybody. For one thing, if you are a pay-per-placement client – that's all you get – you just get media. That means no strategy development, marketing or other work that many authors may need for an effective PR campaign. And if you're not branded correctly, you won't get media – or the right media – anyway.

The costs of a typical "pay-per-placement" program are:

Broadcast Media Interview
National TV = $3,500.00 (network)
National TV = $1,500.00 (Christian)
National Radio = $1,000.00
Satellite Radio = $750.00
Local TV = $500.00
Local Radio = $350.00 ($100 additional for promos/contests)

Print Media (either book review or mention – full features are an additional $250)
Newspapers or Magazines
Circulation 1M+ = $750.00
Circulation 100,001 - 1M = $600.00
Circulation under 10,000 - 100,000 = $500.00

What materials are needed get started?
- Digital photos & other marketing materials
- Copies of recent media coverage
- 10 copies of your book/video/DVD
- Your biography or CV
- Copies of all news releases issued in the last 12 months
- Scripts of any speeches delivered over the past year
- Notes on what you regard as the most newsworthy events in the foreseeable future
- Endorsements you have received

Clients must approve the media MMS delivers – or they don't pay. Our unique guarantee means they pay only for results – PLUS if they are dissatisfied with those results, we will refund the entire placement fee.

We're backed by the experience and contacts that come from over 20 years in the industry. We have had experience generating major media coverage for clients ranging from Essence and Ebony to radio tours in local markets. Our niche is in the African-American Christian market, and if that's your target then it's a good match. If not, the program won't work.

The Difference and Synergy between Advertising and Public Relations

When you pay the media directly – you know exactly when that ad will air or be published. With pay-per-placement, you'll be notified but it's not guaranteed – thus you're not billed until you get the media hit.

PR is not an exact science and you are really at the mercy of the media. It's free when they cover you but you never know when or if they will.

The best formula is to buy ads in publications or on stations that are targeting your audience best – and then pitch the editors/producers too. You'll at least have exposure in the publication or on the station that hits your main audience. Sometimes you'll get favor by being an advertiser and the station or publication will call on you for editorial contributions as well.

The key to any successful promotional campaign is persistence and consistency. Whatever structure you use for your book, make sure you know the expectations and limitations of each one. The most important thing is to find the program that fits your lifestyle, budget and brand.

Joshua's Blueprint for YOUR Success…Revealed

By Anthony & Crystal Obey

"Every place that the sole of your foot will tread upon I have given you, as I said to Moses…No man shall be able to stand before you all the days of your life; as I was with Moses, so I will be with you. I will not leave you nor forsake you. Be strong and very courageous, that you may observe to do according to all the law which Moses My servant commanded you; do not turn from it to the right hand or to the left, that you may prosper wherever you go. This Book of the Law shall not depart from your mouth, but you shall meditate in it day and night, that you may observe to do according to all that is written in it. For then you will make your way prosperous, and then you will have good success. Have I not commanded you? Be strong and of good courage; do not be afraid, nor be dismayed, for the Lord your God is with you wherever you go."

Joshua 1: 3, 5-9

Why claim small things? Why go after small victories? You've only got one life to live; do you really want to live it in a lukewarm, barely scraping by, don't want to ruffle any feathers, I'm too scared to fail kind of way? Naked you came into this world but you need to plan on leaving this world absolutely loaded with unspeakable spiritual jewels, trophies, rewards, riches, and recompense in heaven because of how you lived for God and served Him on Earth.

One thing that really scares me is the thought of getting to my mansion in heaven and finding a room called 'Unclaimed Possessions' which is filled with all these great things that I had access to. I don't want to see all the power I could have used, all the promises I failed to claim, all the victories I failed to gain, and all the underutilized riches that Jesus died on the cross for me to experience right now that have collected dust because I failed to pull them out.

Your Simple Strategy for Ultimate Success

Joshua laid out the master plan or blueprint to success that we've implemented into our lives and is proving to serve us very well. If you're not using this powerful yet simple plan to build the successful life, business, and/or ministry God has called you to then you need to get in on this right now!

Success Strategy #1

Make God your number one Partner and CEO! Jesus died and rose again so that you and I can be joint-heirs with Jesus in everything. We lack nothing in Christ and we're unspeakably rich. Therefore we should never be satisfied with lack, less, poverty, or defeat. God wants to bless you and get the glory from the success of your business and/or ministry, your finances, your health, your relationships, and everything else. So make Him the Captain of your whole life, heart, mind, and soul. Joshua 1: 7-8 tells us the number one way to truly making God the 'Joint Venture Partner' He wants to be in your life. He tells us to observe the Word, meditate on, talk about it, live and breathe it. Then it will penetrate our heart, soul, and mind so that it can then direct our thoughts, build our vision, give us wisdom and discernment in all our dealings, and even help us develop the habits of the highly successful.

The late, Napoleon Hill studied the lives of the richest men of his day and after decades of research he named his legendary book "Think and Grow Rich." How rich is God? What great thoughts does He think? Well, the Word tells us that we have the 'mind of Christ!' We actually have God living inside of us seeking to help us live a life that reflects the mind and thoughts and purposes and powers of Christ.

Success Strategy #2

Trust in Him completely! You must hold on to the promises He made to you. (Joshua 1: 9) He exhorts us over and over again to be strong and courageous knowing that we will inevitably be tempted to throw in the white towel of defeat when met with difficulties that drag us too far out of our comfort zone. So He says to be strong and courageous and not to be afraid and weak because He is with us wherever we go.

He said this but the problem is that most of us struggle to believe it when the bills are coming past due and the business hasn't picked up. It's hard to believe when you've invested all you have including your time, money, creativity, passion, and everything else into building a business or ministry and it still fails to grow as fast as you want it to. So now you're supporting and feeding the vision while the vision is sucking you dry, driving you into debt and depression. God knew that's exactly what Joshua would face because all successful people have had to face their fears. If you read the biographies of some of the richest, most powerful, most successful entrepreneurs it's so funny to find out how many of them went bankrupt on the road to their financial breakthrough.

No matter how hard it gets and how afraid you get, do it afraid! You may feel like you're all alone in a world that won't give back to you what you're putting in but remember that He's with you and He's setting you up for a breakthrough. Always trust Him and seek Him through prayer, studying the word, reading good books like this one, sharing with others you've been there and done that, taking care of your emotions, being good to your body, and cultivating a well-rounded and victorious lifestyle.

Success Strategy #3

Never stop growing and expanding! God said, "Every place that the sole of your foot will tread upon I have given you, as I said to Moses." What's more, the Father told His Son Jesus that He has all power and authority in Heaven and in the Earth and we're joint-heirs with Jesus! So why would any one of us fail to do those 'greater things than these' Jesus said we would be able to do because He was going to His Father? That promise penetrated my heart when I first read it and if you let it penetrate yours you will look up with the eyes of your heart and see a land flowing with milk and honey and endless possibilities for you! Never give up on what you know in your heart is your land because God's already given it to you; it's supposed to be yours, it's always been yours and it always will be.

Get Your Free Gifts Available at SynergyEnergyMarketing.com

Top 10 Tips for Free Publicity

By Pam Perry

1. Send news releases regularly about new products and services, events, contests and awards.

2. Write "how-to" articles for newspapers, magazines, trade publications and newsletters to position yourself as an expert. Load them up in article directories like EzineArticles.com

3. Get onto the speaking circuit. Join NSA (National Speakers Association)

4. Create a web site or blogsite that offers free advice, reciprocal links, articles by and about you and a list of experts (other authors) the media can contact.

5. Publish an electronic newsletter or Ezine packed with free content. Journalists often subscribe to these if the topic interests them.

6. Get to know reporters. Offer yourself as someone they can call on for background, commentary and story ideas. Call and ask, "How can I help you?" (find them in the Christian Writer's Market Guide too)

7. Start your own TV show on your local cable TV company's public access channel. Air time is free. Contact your cable TV company for details.

8. Look for photo opportunities. Local newspapers, TV stations, weekly shoppers, trade publications and other media are always looking for interesting photo opportunities.

9. Give free classes and demonstrations through adult ed programs, at schools and colleges, or at your own business.

10. Participate in online discussion groups and offer lots of helpful advice. Reporters often lurk here, and contact people who they want to quote in articles.

Bonus tip: Google "Christian Writer's Groups" in yahoo and join
www.ChocolatePagesNetwork.com

How to Maximize Your Partnership with God

By Anthony & Crystal Obey

"And if children [of God], then heirs – heirs of God and joint heirs with Christ, if indeed we suffer with Him, that we may also be glorified together." **Romans 8: 17 NKJV**

God created the heavens, the earth, and the entire universe and all that is in it. He created everything seen and unseen. The sheer span of the universe is far too great for us to ever possibly comprehend. There's absolutely no better partner that an ambitious entrepreneur could have, besides Him who loved us so much that He sent His one and only Son, Whom He loved, to be crucified on a cross for our sake! He did it all and paid the price so we could be restored to our great position, so we could once again gain access to the immeasurable wealth we have in Him, and so that we could redeem the intimate relationship we were meant to have.

Most experts agree that you earn within 10% of the top 6 people you spend the most time with. These are the people that give you the mental conditioning that either prepares you for success or failure. Birds of a feather flock together. When we didn't have a lot of people to hang around with we spent time together nurturing our marriage relationship and our dreams. We couldn't get great business advice from a lot of people around us, not necessarily because they didn't love us or care, but because they've never done what we were doing. So we spent and still spend a lot of time with God, learning His ways, His thoughts, His promises, what pleases Him, and His path for our success in business and life.

When you don't have anybody else and even when you do have highly successful people around who can help you move forward, progress, get better, and take your game to the next level, you still need to make God your number one Partner to ensure success beyond your wildest dreams. Here's several ways you should go about doing this.

Commit Your Work to God, Daily

It's not a law but many of the most successful Christians of all time start each day by seeking God. The greatest king of all time, King David, said, "In the morning, O Lord, you hear my voice - in the morning I lay my requests before you and wait in expectation." (Psalm 5: 3) When a pregnant woman is due soon we say she's 'expecting.' If you want to live an 'expectant' life and birth great things then it would be wise to start each day laying all of your requests, concerns, cares, and affairs of your day and life to the Lord.

It's ok to do it in the evening because, again, this is not law. But we've seen the difference in our lives when we start off each day seeking the Lord in prayer, bible study, devotion, and praise. By seeking God each morning before you get all tied up into the knots of the cares of this world you're demonstrating your commitment, your faith, and your love for Him by putting Him first. You're offering Him the first-fruit of the day and God says that if you seek Him first, and His righteousness, He will give you all the things you need and want. I can guarantee your success, prosperity, and fruitfulness in all of your endeavors if you seek God daily.

Learn God's Ways

Moses was one of the greatest men who ever lived. He begged God at one point before going to the next level in his life to show His ways. To learn the ways of God you've got to not only study the word and seek God in prayer but you must also seek God in life! You've got to live with your eyes to the sky; chasing after God like Moses chased God in the wilderness. Learning God's ways comes through experiencing Him. You only experience God when you step out on God's promises and trust

Him to order your steps. You've got to step out of the boat like Peter did when he walked on water. Peter was learning the ways of God, the power of God, the depth of God, and strength of God. It's when you've been knocked down and nobody else is there to pick you up and then God comes in from seemingly nowhere and plants your feet back on solid ground that you begin to learn the ways of God.

Build Integrity and Character

Nothing will sabotage your success and kill your dreams faster than being double-minded, backsliding, and making the wrong decisions. David suffered many deep pains in his life and generations afterwards because of one stupid decision; sleeping with Bathsheba and killing her husband to hide it. What was he thinking?

He got caught up in pride, thinking that he had become invincible. Success can be so intoxicating that it can dull your reasoning skills, cause you to lower your guard, and lead you down the path of disaster. That's why developing integrity and character are so important. It took character for Joseph to refuse the boss's wife when she threw herself at him. It took character for him to sit in prison for years for being falsely accused for doing right when it was probably already difficult for him to resist this temptation. Integrity is about being pure – like refined gold.

You want the great person that people see at church to be the same person when you're out in Las Vegas and you know that 'what happens here, stays here.' Every secret sin, every bad habit, every contradictory belief that you hold in your heart undermines your success. Watch your thoughts, watch what you say, watch how you treat people, and even watch what you watch on a daily basis and you will find that you still need God's help with developing integrity and character.

By doing these things you will be setting yourself up and positioning yourself for success, wealth, health, great relationships, a great self-image, and being the best person God intends for you to be. If you work at something long enough you'll eventually get what you want. But by doing these things you'll get it with far less strife and you'll be able to have peace and enjoy it for the rest of your life with God being your number one partner.

How to Get a Mentor and How to Be a Mentor

By Pam Perry

"Wisdom determines the success of your life. There are two ways to receive Wisdom: mistakes or mentors. Mentors are the difference between poverty and prosperity; decrease and increase; loss and gain; pain and pleasure; deterioration and restoration." **Mike Murdock**

I know the value of mentoring. I have had several mentors in my career – and treasure them all. My mentors have given me wisdom, encouragement and direction. They have propelled my success and continue to influence me to this day. They are my inspiration and I would do anything in the world for them!

That's what good protégés do (that's the secret to having a good mentor). Be willing to give before you get. The more you put into the relationship – the more you will get out of it.

I have had mentors that I've had lunch with, one's that I've house sat for, some that I just read about and even a few I just follow on the internet. But the results are all the same – they are adding value to my life and I am a person who is "in their corner" who is speaking well of them, supporting them and following wherever they lead.

My mentors are people I just "clicked" with upon first meeting them. Sometimes a mentor finds you – but most times you know in your spirit who is assigned by God to mentor, train and teach you some things. A mentor does not have to be anyone famous but they do have to have what ever you lack and are willing to share.

My first mentor was a TV producer, another mentor a publicist, another an advertising manager and another an author. Now at the time I was being mentored by them (in their space) I was serving them. Yes, I was like Ruth to Naomi or Elijah to Elisha. I had no idea that their "anointing" would rub off on me and I would become an Emmy-Award winning TV producer, stellar publicist, ad agency owner and now – an author.

What you make happen for others, God will make happen for you! I'm a witness.

So how do you find a mentor?
1. Conferences
2. School events / careers days
3. Online or in a book

How do you approach a mentor? Very humbly. I wrote my mentor and asked what I could do to help them. Once I was in their space, I just asked them every question I could. I know they probably thought I was so "green" but they we happy to share and impart their wisdom.

You can also get mentored by buying all of the products and participating in all of the programs that a mentor has. I have found that as I "studied" a certain mentor, I began to really know them. Then one day I had the opportunity to meet them in person and they were really impressed with the depth of knowledge I had learned from them.

How to be a mentor?
- Be willing to share you gift with a willing protégé
- Coach – don't ignore faults.
- Give them advice and contacts when they've earned trust.
- Don't be their friend, tell them their weaknesses when you see them

- Keep them accountable by giving them assignments with deadlines (this is also a test to see if the protégé is ready to be mentored) As the old adage says, "When the student is ready, the teacher appears."

What makes a good or "uncommon" protégé? These are from the words of my mentor, Mike Murdock:

- The Uncommon Protégé will Invest Everything to stay in the presence of The Uncommon Mentor.
- The Uncommon Protégé Reveals The Secrets And Dreams Of His Heart With The Mentor.
- The Uncommon Protégé Freely Discusses His Mistakes And Pain With The Mentor.
- The Uncommon Protégé Defines Clearly His Expectations To The Mentor.
- The Uncommon Protégé Gladly Sows Seeds Of Appreciation Back Into The Life Of The Mentor.
- The Uncommon Protégé Ultimately Receives The Mantle Of The Mentor He Serves. Transference of anointing is a fact not a fantasy.
- The Uncommon Protégé Follows The Counsel Of The Uncommon Mentor.
- The Uncommon Protégé Moves Toward The Shelter of The Mentor During A Season Of Uncommon Attack And Warfare.
- The Uncommon Protégé Will Change His Own Schedule To Invest Time In The Presence Of The Mentor.
- The Uncommon Protégé is someone who discerns, respects and pursues the answers God has stored in The Mentor for their life.

Relationships grow us up. Divine relationships stretch us. Covenant connections, though God-inspired, can mirror our frailties and put a microscope on our defects. Don't you just hate that?

Those who know us the most tend to agitate us more. My pastor often says, "Don't hate on your help." He's right. Don't give me a hard time if I'm only trying to help you. It will sting for a minute but it is the medicine you need to make you better.

I have found that many young people I mentor quickly turn sour when corrected or pushed to do more than I know they are capable. If I didn't care, I would let them stay mediocre and substandard. But because I know that they can be more and do more, I drive them. Yes, I'm hated at times – yet envied of my success.

I have achieved my measure of success because I had mentors in my life that didn't let me sleep on the job. I have had relationships that were also a source of agitation because I couldn't just slouch, be lazy or hide. Those persons were apt to scold me, embarrass me and make me take a real hard look at myself. Ouch.

We either learn by mentors or mistakes. Those with a "pride" issue usually learn by mistakes. I have learned to humble myself and listen to my mentors. Yeah, sometimes they make me mad – but I know they know more than me so I listen – and learn.

When God assigns you to a person to "shadow" or to mentor you – don't hate them – imitate them. As my mentor often says, "some things in life can't be taught, they have to be caught." Catch the lessons and enjoy the blessings. God does take foolish things to confound the wise.

Get Your Free Gifts Available at SynergyEnergyMarketing.com

How to Flood Your Business with Eager Clients in Any Economy!

By Anthony & Crystal Obey

"If you're attacking your market from multiple positions and your competition isn't, you have all the advantage and it will show up in your increased success and income." **Jay Abraham**

No wide-eyed entrepreneur ever got into business thinking that they would end up in an even more frustrating version of the "rat race" they experienced as an employee. Nevertheless, after a few lean years of struggling to get by and waiting for the "phones to ring" some business owners are forced to "cry uncle," fold their tent, and once again become a hired hand!

Why do most business owners seem to struggle, beg, and claw to get new customers and turn them into loyal, frequent patrons while a seemingly 'elite and privileged few' seem to set up shop and look on as the widgets fly off the shelves while simultaneously flooding their bank account with cold, hard cash?

Most spectators and business owners alike believe that it's all about location, location, location. "If I build my store on the right corner, they will come!" Many others believe that the secret to skyrocketing sales is having superior products or services. "If my widget is better, they will come!" And most think that they gain a competitive advantage by offering the best widget at the cheapest price. "If I undercut everyone else and am willing to barely get by, they will see my sacrifice and they will come!"

Sure location helps a business…offering better products and services are good too…and sometimes a good liquidation sale can bring in a swarm of bottom-feeders. Sure all these things are good but do you want to know what the single most important, jealously guarded, and little known secret to getting a flood of customers beating your door down and ringing your phones off the hook 24/7, 365 is???

Direct Response M-A-R-K-E-T-I-N-G!

As Direct Response Copywriters we help our small to mid-sized business clients set up automated marketing and response management systems that literally bring in floods of blazing hot new leads and new clients through print ads, direct mail, and online marketing and emotional response copywriting.

Have you ever read a sales letter, free report, or ad in the newspaper that grabbed you and practically pulled the money out of your wallet? Have you ever watched an infomercial that made an offer that was so good you just couldn't refuse it?

Well, most often, the people behind those great ads are not the actual business owners tapping into their new-found salesmanship, in most cases they've hired a good Direct Response Marketer/Copywriter to research their target market, help them plan a winning and unique marketing approach, and write emotionally driven sales copy that grabs their prospects interest and draws them in.

Most small business owners place ads that go right for the sale. But with the rising costs of advertising, you need to use your ad space in a way that the savvy 1% of small business owners do – to simply generate leads of interested prospects, not to get people to just "Buy Now."

Here's the Basic Blueprint for Getting Your Prospects Calling You…

1. Identify your target market and what they want the most

2. Identify where they are/ how you can reach them as fast as possible, and inexpensively

3. Place your ad offering them free gifts such as a Report, CD, DVD, etc.

4. Collect their contact information before you give them the free gift

5. Some will buy based on your educational Free Report, CD, or DVD – Everyone else becomes a lead that you follow up with weekly, monthly, quarterly or as often as you possibly can so as to continue converting those leads into happy customers

This 'blueprint' is simplified due to space but let me tell you that this is "THE" way that nobodies build highly successful businesses seemingly overnight! We've seen it happen and we're helping our clients do it. If you apply Direct Response Marketing and Copywriting to your business by learning it yourself or hiring people like us to help you, you can literally skyrocket your sales. And yes, my friend, "they WILL come!"

How to Manage a Crisis and Position Yourself to Be an Expert

By Monica Wood

"Let all things be done decently and in order." **The Bible (1 Corinthians 14:40)**

More often than not, no one thinks about a crisis until they are already deep in the middle of one. And, then the panic button is pushed.

What I am about to say is not new news….but, yet, we continue to be the unfortunate beneficiary of poor or absent planning. The best time to plan for a crisis is always before you are in a crisis. The smartest thing any company, organization, author, athlete, etc. could ever do is to include or at least have on the radar some resemblance of a Crisis Plan within their overall Communications Strategy or Business Plan. This is especially true, if you already know that your product or message is controversial itself.

Don't let the crisis have the upper hand. When you allow a crisis to manage you, you are instantly put in a defensive stance. You are reacting to what is being thrown at you and you are often rarely prepared to strategically and intelligently respond.

But, with a crisis plan in place, YOU immediately have the upper hand and play strategic offense. You are already prepared with rehearsed and clear and concise responses. And, with that, you are able to lessen the blow or at least take the sting out of the initial punch.

Although you can never be totally prepared for the unknown, you can have a playbook to refer to with all possible scenarios addressed, for the "just in case."

What is a crisis?

A general description of a crisis is anything that threatens the well-being of you, your product or message. As it pertains to the Christian community, a crisis can be anything from the Rev. Jeremiah Wright ordeal to a racy title of a "Christian" novel where real names or situations are used.

A crisis could be characterized by one or more of the following:
- You lose control over outside variables.
- Public attention to an issue escalates, most often in response to media interest.
- The issue involves a highly visible special interest group.
- The issue is based on a well-prepared attack by a national organization.
- The issue has potential for sustained media interest.
- Your product or message itself is controversial in nature.

What do you do when a crisis occurs?

When a crisis occurs, you are judged on the way you respond. Which means it is important to not delay your response. And, to be as concise, consistent and clear as you can out the gate. How one communicates to all constituents determines if a crisis can be controlled or if it will take on a life of its own.

So, for example, do not let your first response come on Sunday morning from the pulpit…it will make matters worse. Rather attempt to do the following:

1. Stay calm.
2. Tell the truth.

3. Tell only what you know.
4. Admit what you don't know and explain why.
5. Keep it simple and sweet. (KISS it)
6. Show compassion.
7. Don't speculate.
8. Keep consistent message.

How do you handle the press?

Although, your initial reaction might be to jump in front of the mic and defend yourself, you can't. Again, it is important to say the right thing, the first time. Remember that you are in the driver's seat. You set the tone and the direction in which the crisis will go with the media. Even though it is important to tell your story before it is told for you elsewhere, you must first collect the facts and identify the most qualified person (i.e. a PR professional or publicist) to help shape your message, if not deliver the message on your behalf.

It can never be stated too much that when it is time to speak, be sure you connect emotionally, that you tell the truth, that you act quickly, take responsibility, control facts and rumors, keep your message simple and focus only on the facts as you know them at the time. Let the media feel that what you are telling them is all there is, gaining their just as well as deterring them from going on their own fact-finding mission.

The way you handle your crisis will determine how many allies (media, community, etc.) you have on your team in the future. Always keep that in mind as you mange through the murky waters of a crisis. Because once the dust clears, these are the same folks you will look to proactively approach one day with your own agenda, be it a message, event, product or service.

How to position yourself as an expert?

Haven't you ever wondered how a particular individual got the title of "expert" on a news program? Why did the media call on them? Truly they know that you are more of an expert than THAT person. Well, actually, they do not. Why, because they do not know you exist.

If something happens that impacts an area that is familiar to you, you can position yourself as a resource (expert) to speak on that issue and help the media shape their story. I feel bad in saying this, but you, like them can benefit from someone else's pain.

However, even in that scenario, you must prepare in advance. Create press kits and distribute them to targeted media outlets introducing yourself, your product, your service or expertise. Develop relationships with them, to keep you top of mind. And, when that unfortunate day comes, reach out to them and remind them of your background and offer them your perspective. And, let someone else sit at home or in their office asking the screen, "How did they get to be an 'expert'?"

Monica Wood is president of MWPR, Inc. and co-partner of Off-The-Field Branding: Personal and Professional Management, LLC. She has been brought in to conduct crisis management workshops for several organizations. Her specialty is in sports and faith brand/reputation management. To learn more visit her blog www.mwprinsight.blogspot.com as well as her website www.mwprinc.com.

The Missing Link to Quickly Skyrocketing Your Sales…Guaranteed!

By Anthony & Crystal Obey

"Great copy is the heart and soul of the advertising business, whether it's for print, television, radio, or any other medium."
The Adweek Copywriting Handbook

Arguably, one of the biggest single issues that entrepreneurs have when launching their new venture and even growing it is the failure to truly understand the power of direct response marketing and gaining basic copywriting skills. It matters very little if you've built a beautiful restaurant, with a 5 star meal selection, a warm and inviting atmosphere, and first-class customer service if you don't get enough bums in seats everyday to keep the lights on, pay your debts, and sneak away with a decent income to live on. Why does a local McDonalds generate millions of dollars each year while many boutique restaurants that offer fine, organic cuisine go belly up all around these fast food burger joints? McDonalds understands marketing which begins and ends with understanding their target market.

Direct Response Marketing is the discipline of effectively delivering goods and services to a targeted group of prospects and measuring the results of each advertisement.

We get clients who come to us wanting to increase sales and get a marketing makeover for their business and the first thing we do before we write sales copy for their business is assess what their target market wants. Your business will rise and fall based on your ability to effectively communicate that you have exactly what this group of people wants, and delivering exactly that. In other words, most businesses are only operating at a small fraction of their capacity. What's worse is that most business owners fail to communicate the message of what their business offers to their target market. It's not that most businesses aren't good enough, it's that their marketing campaigns aren't!

Marketing is the life-blood of any business because marketing brings in the customers through which any enterprise grows. No customers, no money – no money, no business! You can be a great accountant, a great cook, offer great customer service, and all of that but if you don't know how to market you're doomed in business. If you've got great sales copy on everything from your business cards, brochures, and phone book ads to your newspaper ads, direct mail, and websites that works cohesively together to lead people into making a buying decision, then we can almost guarantee your success.

Here's 9 of the Most Important Elements of Any Effective Marketing or Promotional Piece

Element #1 Headline

The headline is one of the most important parts of any sales piece because it gets the attention of the reader and identifies what you're talking about, what's in it for them, how what you're offering will improve their life, etc. A good headline on the homepage of your website can be 5 to 10 times bigger than the normal text because it captures your audience immediately. Always make a big bold promise in your headline and always put it in quotes.

Element #2 Identify the Problem, Pain, or Frustration

Most people are more likely to do things to avoid pain rather than improve their life; that's a fact. So a headline like, "The 5 Biggest Mistakes Most People Make When Choosing a Cosmetic Surgeon and How to Avoid Them!" is a powerful headline because it shows people who are interested in cosmetic surgery that there are some potentially devastating consequences associated with failing to read on. But you must also identify the problem in order to let your prospect know that you've been where they are and you know how to overcome their predicament.

Element #3 Agitate the Problem

Once you've identified the problem you should then go on to provide stories of people who've had the problem as well as quotes, statistics, case studies and other facts that pull at the emotional strings of the prospect and magnify the dilemma.

Element #4 Solution to Problem

This is where you burst in saying, "Have no fear, Wonder Dog is here!" This is where you offer your product or service as the perfect solution to their problem; the perfect remedy to their pain; the most revolutionary way to solving their problem better than anything before it. You shouldn't lie or be short-sighted about other possible solutions but you must establish your unique way of solving the problem in a way that no one else can compete with.

Element #5 USP

This is you unique selling proposition (USP). This is what sets you apart. This is what makes you different, superior, advanced, and far better than the rest. Wal-Mart's USP is "Everyday low prices, always." This may take you some time to develop but you cannot expect to thrive if you're just like everybody else.

Element #6 Proof

You can't just say you're better and that you can solve their problem, you've got to prove it. Scientific evidence, quotes by industry authorities and experts, statistics and facts, case studies, before and after photos, and detailed testimonials (from experts and common customers) are your proof.

Element #7 Urgency and Scarcity

You've got to set firm deadlines to get people to act fast! You must communicate to them that your offer is only for a limited time and only for a certain number of people; and stick to it. Giving people a deadline and creating scarcity makes them act fast instead of procrastinating.

Element #8 Call to Action

You've got to call people to action, firmly. Many people don't sell as much as they could simply because they're afraid or just forget to tell the prospect what they need to do next to get started or take action. Make a clear, big, and firm call to action in all of sales copy and you'll increase response with this element alone!

Element #9 Close

You need to close out your sales piece and if it's a short or long sales letter you're writing, always include a P.S. Some people will only read the PS to get straight to the bottom-line of what you're talking about. The PS should re-state the offer, call to action, urgency, and scarcity as clearly as possible.

You don't have to do any of this perfectly and you'll increase your response just by doing a half way decent job at it…guaranteed!

Get Your Free Gifts Available at SynergyEnergyMarketing.com

Steps to Positioning/Branding Yourself in the African American Christian Market (AACM)

By Pam Perry

"Any enterprise built by wise planning, becomes strong through common sense, and profits wonderfully by keeping abreast of the facts." Proverbs 24:3-4 TLB

Step 1: Define your target audience.
Who is your main customer? What do they look like? What do they watch? Listen to? What other media do they consume? The more research you do the more you can identify and target your ideal customer to BUY YOUR BOOK!

UNDERSTAND YOUR MARKET… Once you have an idea, research it. Check Amazon and see if any similar books exists. Is there a need for your book? How will your book be different? Will it withstand the competition? Find out everything you can about your topic; become the authority.

Step 2: What's your PLATFORM?
Find your "book hook." What message are you marketing?
Get your message "out there!" But what do you want to say? Are you an expert? An evangelist? Do you want to position yourself as a "brain" or a "creative" – or do you have endorsements that will speak volumes for you? Whoever endorses you will "pin point" how you will be perceived/branded in the market. Make sure your message that you communicate makes the media say "wow" and not yawn. Examine yourself and find your unique selling position. Why is your book worthy of media attention?

Talk to everyone you know, network, get a marketing mindset! Find places to start, get bookings to teach/speak and work your way up. Make your initial mistakes locally, and build a devoted following close to home. Take speaking, voice or acting lessons, or hire a media or PR coach. Join the local Toastmasters or the National Speakers Association. You'll get practice speaking in front of people, feedback and contacts for places to speak. Video yourself; critique yourself; and practice a lot. You want to shine for the media and make your "followers" proud.

Step 3: Build a media "wish list"
We would all love to be on Oprah, Tom Joyner, Steve Harvey and TBN…that's a for sure bestseller status. But starting out, get a focused, realistic media database that reaches the core target audience. What do they read, watch and listen to? Do you really know the media? Google the media that matches your platform.

Look up other authors in your genre and Google them to see where they have had media hits. Put those on your "wish list" and go find those same reporters/stations. No need to buy expensive media lists and do mass mailings – that is old school and doesn't work.

Find addresses at websites. Although websites seldom reveal addresses of print or broadcast contacts, they're a good place to find the addresses of website editors and content producers, and to figure out the company's addressing system. You can sometimes find e-mail addresses using online directories such as Yahoo's People Search. Also, Linkedin.com is a good source. I know tons of authors who have made personal contact with producers through social networking sites like facebook, myspace, or twitter.

Another smart way to find e-mail addresses is to browse the message boards or blog at websites for newspapers, magazines, radio stations, and TV stations. Reporters and producers often respond to comments and criticism on these boards and blogs, and their e-mail addresses are usually displayed along with their messages

Use Eblast services too to "stir up the buzz" and get the word out immediately to the masses.

Here are some Eblast service/media to look at:
(Targeting the African-American and African-American Christian markets)

BlackGospelPromo.com	GospelTruthMagazine.com
DetroitGospel.com	GospelToday.com
GoodGirlBookClubOnline.com	CushCity.com
UrbanGospelPromo.com	UrbanGospelPromo.com
GospelCity.com	GospelFlava.com
BlackBookPromo.com	Rawsistaz.com
UrbanRoundUp.com	MosaicBooks.com (300 BookClubs)
GospelEblast.com	NewYorkGospel.com
GospelEFlyer.com	GospelFruits.com
TheLoopOnline.com	Izania.com
MIProductions.org	BlackChristianbookpromo.com
MinistryMarketingSolutions.com	Gospeltube.com
ChristianPRGroup.com	Blacknews.com

Step 4: Create dazzling press materials.

If you're trying to pitch Essence, "O" magazine or your local weekly neighborhood newspaper, you better come correct. You only have one chance to make a first impression. Get customized press kit folders if doing mailing. Or get graphics help to design your EPK (electronic press kit). But whatever you do, get great author photos. A picture is worth a thousand words – and a "glamour" shot will get you noticed. Even in the Christian market, sex appeal sells. Make sure your press releases, fact sheets, articles and pitch letters stand out from the crowd and "position" yourself. BRAND!

In this electronic age, having a top-notch Website and Electronic Press Kit will show that an author is professional. Increasingly, editors are viewing them as tickets to the game.

Great error-free press materials are the foundation to a good campaign.

Step 5: Media contacts – they are your friends.

How do you meet the media? Go where they go. Go to conferences where you know media will be there like the Gospel Heritage Conference, The PowerNetworking Conference, The Stellar Awards, ICRS (formerly CBA) and even the regional/local National Black Association of Black Journalists. It is not a bad idea to join as an associate member. You're a writer, right? Networking and building relationships is critical. If you can meet them, keep in contact by commenting on their work – so they know you're just not "begging" alllll the time – but really are an educated media consumer. (Also, get their name right!)

When you prove yourself as an "expert" and dependable source of information, you get reporters to contact you over and over. And they will tell their friends about you because you will become known as a good source.

But never brow beat and badger a reporter/producer with unwanted phone calls, faxes or E-mails – that's a quick way to make an enemy with the whole industry. If they don't respond, ask them why and then move on. There are tons of other media that will reach your target market. Use your time and energy wisely and don't be a pain – and when you really have something to contact them about – just a quick email is all that is needed.

FINALLY and most importantly: REMAIN ENCOURAGED, STEADFAST AND prayerful. Prayer is the key.

The Secret to Making Your Website Sell!

By Anthony & Crystal Obey

"People get caught up in wonderful, eye-catching pitches, but they don't do enough to close the deal. It's no good if you don't make the sale. Even if your foot is in the door or you bring someone into a conference room, you don't win the deal unless you actually get them to sign on the dotted line." **Donald Trump**

You may have noticed that the World Wide Web has created the virtual 'haves and have nots.' There are those who practically go from being complete nobodies to seemingly becoming overnight successes with money, huge sales, and massive online presence – and then there are those who've been stuck in the trenches, failing to get traffic to their site; and if they do get traffic to their site, nobody ever buys. Arrrgg!

We work with business owners to create direct response marketing campaigns using proven methods, systems, and strategies that only the 'insiders' know about. Understanding how to get traffic to your site and then convert that traffic into long-term, loyal customers is a matter of marketing, and that's why internet marketers and copywriters are the invisible driving force behind effective e-commerce. We'll share a few of the foundational secrets that some pay hundreds to learn themselves and thousands to have an expert implement for them.

5 Keys to Skyrocketing Your Site Sales

Key #1 Build a Content Website

It's not called the "Products & Services Highway" it's called the "Information Highway!" The majority of people don't go online to buy stuff; they go there to search and to learn. It's not that they won't buy, it's just that they don't log on intending to be sold by your products or services. So it's fundamentally counterproductive for you to build a website that's nothing more than a storefront. Think about it – what are the most popular websites online? Social networking sites and informational, educational, content sites that provide accurate and helpful information for free.

These sites provide something free on the front-end but they make money on the back-end when you click on their Google ads, affiliate links, and finally purchase their products and services. And why did you buy from them? Because you trust them, see them as experts, and you're hanging out there all the time!

That's what a real 'sticky' site is all about - providing high-quality content and giving away great advice that's laced with a soft offer to buy. This builds incredible rapport, trust, and reciprocity with your prospects. And the strategy to maximizing this key is to search engine optimize (SEO) each of the content pages on your website so that Google, Yahoo, MSN, and other search engines direct traffic to your site.

There are people who build 300 SEO page sites that Google rewards by driving 50,000 + unique visitors to their site each month. These sites rake in the cash! Type in any key word like 'colon cleanse' and the first 10 resulting sites are those that have mastered SEO site building.

Key #2 Write Content that Convinces Prospects that You're the Expert

Becoming the expert in your field is one of the premiere positioning strategies that's been used for decades if not centuries to drive business to these savvy business people. Real internet marketing masters know how to write persuasive content that pre-sells their prospect. That's what we do as copywriters – we write sales copy for online, print, and direct mail marketing campaigns.

Copywriters are the backbone to selling online because they serve as a webmaster's 'virtual salesman.' Well written content on your website can dramatically skyrocket your sales while poorly written sales copy will turn people off, scare them away, or just confuse them.

Key #3 Develop Product & Service Offerings

Now we're finally at the point where we should be talking about making some cash. Notice that first we've built a strong content website to begin generating search engine traffic through SEO content pages. Next, we've made sure that each of those pages, but especially pages that sell our products & services, are professionally written using good copywriting technique to persuade, convince, and entice people to buy from us. Now we're finally ready to make some money! You have to understand that a well-built website doesn't have to sell only one business's services, products, or represent one business. Your goal should be to build a strong site that generates a lot of traffic so that you can build a large list.

The people who make the most money online are not the ones who merely convert traffic into sales initially, because that just won't happen in big numbers. Sure, you're going to convert a percentage of your initial traffic into sales, especially if you've got great sales copy selling your products & services. But the most important thing you can understand in converting visitors into customers is that most won't buy initially. That's why you must collect their email address and email them regularly through an automated contact management system. This allows you to build a massive list that you can send out email promotions to forever, converting more and more of this list into buying customers. Your site is nothing but a vehicle to build your list. So then, the real asset is not the website, but the list! Marketers brag about having a list of 200,000 names on it because that means they've got that many prospects who they're converting into customers one email at a time!

Key #4 Create a Consistent and Professional Look & Feel

Some people get a little too carried away with this one. Nobody is going to buy anything from your site just because it's all 'purrrtey!' You can have an artsy-fartsy, fancy, flashing website that looks beautiful and slick. It can have one of those cute intro pages and other bells and whistles and you still won't necessarily convert any visitor into a buying customer. As a matter of fact, you may scare away a lot of internet browsers who are looking for what? FREE content, not pretty sites. You should have a nice look & feel to your website that's consistent with your theme, message and purpose of your site but any marketer will tell you that images, logos, and beautiful design work will distract your prospects and scare them away unless the image directly strengthens your message. The more white space you have on your site, the better. Visitors' eyes should be drawn to your content and nothing does this better than a white background and black words!

The better you learn these foundational keys to website sales success, the more money you'll make and the more you will understand that there are truly unlimited streams of income to be had by understanding and implementing internet marketing techniques.

APPENDIX

PUBLICITY RESOURCES

There are many excellent ways to build a media list that is best targeted to a given book and author. Here are some of the tools publishers, authors, and book publicists often use. All are available for sale, and many are available in library reference rooms, but libraries don't always have the current editions.

Bacon's Media Directories (now Cision)
http://us.cision.com/products_services/bacons_media_directories_2008.asp
These directories include in-depth profiles on more than 150,000 reporters, editors, and columnists. You can search for the reporters and outlets of most interest to you and create customized media lists by publication, market, beat, or other criteria. Options include: *Newspaper/Magazine Directory*, *Radio/TV/Cable Directory*, *Media Calendar Directory*, *Internet Media Directory* ($425 each set, found in many library reference rooms), *New York Publicity Outlets Directory*, and *Metro California Media Directory* ($375 each). Bacon's lists online include 80,000 media outlets and more than 600,000 individual reporters, editors, columnists, and freelancers, so you can quickly build customized media lists that are accurate and on target with your goals. Each media contact is 70¢; there is a $100 minimum charge per order.

The Gale Database of Publications and Broadcast Media
http://www.gale.cengage.com/DirectoryLibrary/
This premier media directory contains thousands of listings for radio and television stations and cable companies. Print media entries provide address, phone, fax numbers, and email addresses; key personnel, including feature editors; and much more. Broadcast media entries provide address, phone, fax, and email addresses; key personnel; owner information; hours of operation; networks carried; and more ($950).

All-in-One Media Directory
www.gebbiepress.com
Gebbie Press products include an annual *All-in-One Media Directory*, print version ($155) and an annual *All-in-One Media Directory*, data-only CD versions: Daily and Weekly Newspaper CD, Radio and Television CD, and Trade and Consumer Magazines CD ($155 each, $415.00 for all three). **Gebbie also sells an annual *All-In-One Media Directory, PR Pro* CD software ($565).**

Harrison's Guide to the Top National TV Talk and Interview Shows
www.freepublicity.com
Contains detailed profiles of over **600 key contacts at more than 280 top national cable and TV shows that interview guests** ($267–$497, depending on options).

Dan Poynter's Para-Publishing
www.parapublishing.com
Many reports, lists, and other products and services.

Bonus Code = Together

Book Marketing Update
www.bookmarket.com

This twice-monthly subscription newsletter is edited by John Kremer (author of *1001 Ways to Market Your Book*) and produced by Bradley Communications (*Radio TV Interview Report*; *www.rtir.com*). It keeps you up to date on key media contacts where you can get free publicity for your book ($227 at the one-year author/small press rate).

PartyLine
www.expertclick.com

This media placement newsletter is a weekly roundup of opportunities. It's available by email only ($167.50 per year).

Bulldog Reporter
www.bulldogreporter.com

Bulldog issues *Lifestyle Media* and *Business Media* bimonthly newsletters ($449 each per year) and *National PR Pitch Books* media directories. The directories include contact information on the 43,000 most influential journalists and 30,000 top media in the United States—plus Bulldog Reporter's exclusive PitchingTips, which give details on how these journalists want and don't want to be pitched. Its volumes cover *Business and Consumer*; *Health, Fitness and Medicine*; *Investment, Banking and Financial Services*; *Travel, Food and Hospitality*; and *Issues, Politics and Policy* ($450–$499 each). Bulldog also offers custom list-building. Prices vary from $195 base price plus $7/name for its Master List of unusual subjects or when traditional beat definitions aren't precise enough, to $195 base price plus $3/name for its Express list, when your story topic or press release matches traditional beats.

ProfNet
info.prnewswire.com, information@prnewswire.com, *or 888/776-0942*

Links reporters quickly and conveniently with expert sources.

Gordon's Radio List
www.radiopublicity.net, *or 949/855-0640*

This list provides contact information for more than 1,100 radio shows that interview authors and other guests. It includes hosts' and producers' names, addresses, e-mails, and phone and fax numbers, plus notes on what each show is about. Unlike other lists, it is updated daily. Results are also guaranteed; William Gordon will investigate any listing that appears to be out of date and report back to you. Available in Word or Excel for $329.

Joe Sabah's Radio List
www.sabahradioshows.com

A *Current Database of 953 Radio Talk Shows Who Interview Guests by Telephone* includes call letters of the station, name of the show, hosts' and producers' names, address, phone and fax numbers, Watts (power of the station), email addresses, and Web sites. Available on PC or Mac CD in ASCII format, which can be imported into any program with an import feature. *Note:* Joe updates this database every six months, because the turnover in radio stations is so high ($99).

Web Resources

The Web has a lot of media resources, of course. Some are free; some cost. Some give only a little information—company name, address, and basic email address—while others are more detailed. Useful Internet resources include a Media Directory of Local, Daily and Weekly Newspapers at *www.bizmove.com*; and**, for radio stations,** *www.radio-directory.com*. A little searching will lead you to many others. Also go to www.nrb.org (National Religious Broadcasters).

Get Your Free Gifts Available at SynergyEnergyMarketing.com

TOOLS FOR A SUCCESSFUL BOOK CAMPAIGN

You must promote and advertise your book to enhance sales to a specific **target audience.** Publishers can assist but they will not do it for you!

Media to leverage (publicity or advertising) – you must do both!

- Radio
- TV
- Cable shows
- Newspapers
- Magazines
- Online shows (internet TV and Radio)
- Discussion groups
- Elists like: BlackGospelPromo.com, Detroit Gospel.com, Chicagogospel.com, Christianhangsuite.com, BlackBookpromo.com, Goodgirlbookclubonline.com

Promotional tools to use:
- Bookmarks
- Postcards
- Flyers
- CDs
- Premiums or see www.CaféPress.com
- Menus or fan or other "keepers"
- Chapter summary brochure style
- Posters
- Newsletters
- Press Kits

Must have for a press kit:
- Release (Who, What, When, Where, Why)
- Bio & PROFESSIONAL photo
- Book Cover or postcard of cover
- Endorsements
- Author Questions
- One Sheet (similar to bio)
- Book tour schedule
- Other clips or video/audio tapes
- Fact Sheet
- Book Description
- Book Review (optional)

> "The thoughts of the diligent tend only to plenteousness;
> But [those] of every one that is hasty, only to want."
> --Proverbs 21:5

Get Your Free Gifts Available at SynergyEnergyMarketing.com

PUBLISHING SELF-ASSESSMENT
Before you publish, take this test.

1. You have at least $2,500 to $5,000 to invest in the project.

2. Your topic is a topic that is very "marketable" in a book.

3. You regularly support other author events, i.e. book signings and lectures.

4. You frequently visit bookstores and know what the trends are in Christian books and know the best sellers.

5. You have a website or plan to get one to sell/market your book.

6. You've published articles or regularly speak/lecture thereby you have an "audience" for your book.

7. You research and read books/magazines on publishing or go to writer's conferences or are apart of a writer's group.

8. You know a good graphic designer, editor and webmaster – or at least know where to find one.

9. You have a written marketing plan and know how you're going to sell your book– before you've written it.

10. You have at least 10 hours a week to promote your book.

11. You are part a writer's discussion group online or blog regularly.

If you have answered "yes" to 7 or more of these questions, you are a good candidate to be a successful author.

If not, you now have a guideline us to what to do before you start the publishing process.

For more information, visit www.MinistryMarketingSolutions.com and Sign-up for free email marketing and publishing tips, ideas and inspiration. Pam Perry 248.426.2300.

LISTING of CHRISTIAN WRITER'S CONFERENCES

January/Feb: WRITING FOR THE SOUL CONFERENCE*
Colorado Springs CO
Paul Finch
866-495-5177
paul@christianwritersguild.com
www.christianwritersguild.com

February: WRITER'S SYMPOSIUM BY THE SEA
San Diego CA
Dean Nelson
Deannelson@pointloma.edu
www.pointloma.edu/writers

February: WORD WEAVERS RETREAT
Lake Yale Retreat & Conference Center; Leesburg FL
Larry Leech
Lleech@cfl.rr.com

February: AMERICAN CHRISTIAN WRITERS DALLAS CONFERENCE
Dallas TX
Reg Forder
1-800-21-WRITE
ACWriters@aol.com
www.ACWriters.com

February: NATIONAL CHRISTIAN WRITERS CONFERENCE
Antonio L. Crawford
804-998-8014
ncwcbe@yahoo.com
www.nationalchristianwritersconference.com

February: AMERICAN CHRISTIAN WRITERS
Oklahoma City OK
Reg Forder
1-800-21-WRITE
ACWriters@aol.com
www.ACWriters.com

February: CASTRO VALLEY CHRISTIAN WRITERS CONFERENCE
Castro Valley CA
510-886-6300
jdrury@redwoodchapel.org

February: WRITERS WEEK-END AT THE BEACH
Ocean Park WA
Birdie Etchison
360-665-6576
etchison@pacifier.com
www.patriciarushford.com

February: CATHOLIC SCREENWRITERS WORKSHOP
Tucson AZ
Rev. Thomas Santa, CssR
866-737-5751
office@desertrenewal.org
www.desertrenewal.org

Feb/Mar: FLORIDA CHRISTIAN WRITERS CONFERENCE
Billie Wilson,
321-269-5831
billiewilson@cfl.rr.com
www.FLWriters.org

March: HEART TALK/SPEAKING CONFERENCE
Portland OR
Beverly Hislop
503-517-1931
wcm@westernseminary.edu
www.westernseminary.edu/women

March: MOUNT HERMON CHRISTIAN WRITERS CONFERENCE
Mount Hermon CA (near Santa Cruz)
David Talbott
831-335-4466
rachelw@mhcamps.org
www.mounthermon.org/writers

March: AMERICAN CHRISTIAN WRITERS
Memphis TN
Reg Forder
1-800-21-WRITE
ACWriters@aol.com
www.ACWriters.com

March: AMERICAN CHRISTIAN WRITERS
Charlotte NC
Reg Forder
ACWriters@aol.com
www.ACWriters.com

March: INSPIRATIONAL WRITERS ALIVE!
Amarillo TX
Jerry McClenagan
806-355-7117
jerrydalemc@sbcglobal.net

April: JOURNALISM THROUGH THE EYES OF

March/April: WRITE ON! WORKSHOP
Dayton OH
Valerie Coleman
937-307-0760
info@penofthewriter.com
www.penofthewriter.com

April: ORANGE COUNTY CHRISTIAN WRITERS FELLOWSHIP SPRING WRITING DAY
John DeSimone
714-538-7070
John@occwf.org
www.occwf.org

April: BIOLA MEDIA CONFERENCE
LaMirada CA
Craig Detweiler
866-334-2266
www.biolamedia.com

April: CALLED TO WRITE
Girard KS
Deborah Vogts
620-244-5619
debvogts@terraworld.net
www.christianwritersgirard.org

April: AMERICAN CHRISTIAN WRITERS
Baltimore MD
Reg Forder
1-800-21-WRITE
ACWriters@aol.com
www.ACWriters.com

April: QUAD-CITIES CHRISTIAN WRITERS CONFERENCE
Bettendorf IA
Twila Belk
563-332-1622
iamstraightway@aol.com
www.gottatellsomebody.com

April: AMERICAN CHRISTIAN WRITERS
Indianapolis IN
Reg Forder
1-800-21-WRITE
ACWriters@aol.com
www.ACWriters.com

April: MINNESOTA CHRISTIAN WRITERS GUILD SPRING SEMINAR
Minneapolis/St. Paul MN
Delores Topliff 651-695-0609
sharonknudson@hotmail.com
www.mnchristianwriters.org

FAITH
St. Paul MN
Phyllis Alsdurf
651-638-6149
p-alsdurf@bethel.edu
www.bethel.edu/special-events/jtef

April: DELAWARE CHRISTIAN WRITERS CONFERENCE
Newark DE
John Riddle
302-834-4910
Delawarewriter@yahoo.com
www.DelawareChristianWritersConference.com

April: AMERICAN CHRISTIAN WRITERS
Fort Wayne IN
Reg Forder
1-800-21-WRITE
ACWriters@aol.com
www.ACWriters.com

April: WFCA WRITERS CONFERENCE
Milwaukee WI
Andrea Boeshaar/Patti Wolf
414-355-5202
andrea@andreaboeshaar.com
www.wisconsinchristianauthors.com

April: MERCER ONE-DAY WORKSHOP
Mercer PA
Evelyn Minshull or Gloria Clover
724-475-3239 or 724-253-2635
eminshull@certainty.net , or
gloworm@certainly.net
www.stdavidswriters.com

May: INSPIRATIONAL WRITERS ALIVE! EAST TEXAS SEMINAR
Tyler TX
Maxine Holder
903-795-3986
mholder787@aol.com

May: AMERICAN CHRISTIAN WRITERS
Atlanta GA
Reg Forder
1-800-21-WRITE
ACWriters@aol.com
www.ACWriters.com

May: ANTELOPE VALLEY CHRISTIAN WRITERS CONFERENCE
Quartz Hill CA
Don Patterson
661-722-0891
donrpatterson@verizon.net
www.avwriters.com

May:
NORTHWEST CHRISTIAN WRITERS RENEWAL
Bothell WA
Judy Bodmer
425-488-2900
conference@nwchristianwriters.org
www.nwchristianwriters.org

May : GEORGIA WRITERS SPRING FESTIVAL
Atlanta GA
Lloyd Blackwell
(770)421-1203 .
lloydblackwell@worldnet.att.net

May: EVANGELICAL PRESS ASSN. CONVENTION
Portland OR
Doug Trouten
763-535-4793
director@epassoc.org
www.epassoc.org

May: AMERICAN CHRISTIAN WRITERS
Nashville TN
Reg Forder
1-800-21-WRITE
ACWriters@aol.com
www.ACWriters.com

May: COLORADO CHRISTIAN WRITERS CONFERENCE
Estes Park CO
Marlene Bagnull
610-626-6833
mbagnull@aol.com
www.writehisanswer.com

May: BLUE RIDGE MT. CHRISTIAN WRITERS CONFERENCE
Lifeway Ridgecrest Conference Center NC
Ron Pratt
615-251-2065
ron.pratt@lifeway.com

May: AMERICAN CHRISTIAN WRITERS
Louisville KY
Reg Forder
1-800-21-WRITE
ACWriters@aol.com
www.ACWriters.com

June (usual 3rd Weekend): SHE SPEAKS CONFERENCE
Charlotte NC
LeAnn Rice
704-849-2270
office@Proverbs31.org
www.SheSpeaksConference.com

June: ST. DAVIDS CHRISTIAN WRITERS CONFERENCE
Audrey Stallsmith
724-253-2738
registrar@stdavidswriters.com
www.stdavidswriters.com

June: SOUTHERN CHRISTIAN WRITERS CONFERENCE
Tuscaloosa AL
Joanne Sloan
205-333-8603
SCWCworkshop@bellsouth.net

June: FICTION INTENSIVE
Tehachapi CA
Lauraine Snelling
661-823-0669
tlsnelling@yahoo.com
www.laurainesnelling.net

June: WRITE TO PUBLISH CONFERENCE
Wheaton IL (Chicago area)
Lin Johnson
847-296-3964
lin@writetopublish.com
www.WriteToPublish.com

June: AMERICAN CHRISTIAN WRITERS
Columbus OH
Reg Forder
1-800-21-WRITE
ACWriters@aol.com
www.ACWriters.com

June: EAST TEXAS CHRISTIAN WRITERS CONFERENCE
Marshall TX
Dr. Jerry Hopkins 903-923-2269
jhopkins@ETBU.edu
www.ETBU.edu/news/CWC/default.htm

June: ANNUAL ARKANSAS WRITERS CONFERENCE
Little Rock AR
Helen Austin
501-223-8633
hmaustin@comcast.net
www.geocities.com/penwomen

June: CEDAR FALL CHRISTIAN WRITERS WORKSHOP
Riverview Conference Center, Cedar Falls IA
Jean Vaux;
319-231-7761 ;
Vauxcom@cfu.net

June: WESLEYAN WRITERS CONFERENCE
Middletown CT
Anne Greene
860-685-3604
agreene@wesleyan.edu
www.wesleyan.edu/writers

June: AMERICAN CHRISTIAN WRITERS
Grand Rapids MI
Reg Forder
1-800-21-WRITE
ACWriters@aol.com
www.ACWriters.com

June: KENTUCKY CHRISTIAN WRITERS CONFERENCE
Elizabethtown KY
Judy Sliger
Registrar@kychristianwriters.com
www.kychristianwriters.com

July: AMERICAN CHRISTIAN WRITERS
Orlando FL
Reg Forder
1-800-21-WRITE
ACWriters@aol.com
www.ACWriters.com

July: DAYTON CHRISTIAN WRITERS GUILD CONFERENCE
Dayton OH
Tina V. Toles
937-836-6600 : 937-371-6083
Daytonwriters@ureach.com
www.dougtoles.com

July: INTERNATIONAL CHRISTIAN RETAIL SHOW (CBA)
Scott Graham
719-265-9895
sgraham@cbaonline.org
www.christianretailshow.com

July: MONTROSE CHRISTIAN WRITERS CONFERENCE
Montrose PA
Patti Souder
570-278-1001
mbc@montrosebible.org
www.montrosebible.org

July– MIDWEST WRITERS CONFERENCE
Dept. of Journalism
765-282-1055
midwestwriters@yahoo.com
www.midwestwriters.org

July– OREGON CHRISTIAN WRITERS CONFERENCE
Canby OR
www.oregonchristianwriters.org

July/August: THE GLEN WORKSHOP
Gregory Wolfe/Image
206-281-2988
glenworkshop@imagejournal.org
www.imagejournal.org/glen

August: FAITHWRITERS.COM WRITING CONFERENCE
Livonia MI (Detroit Metro area)
Scott Lindsay
support@faithwriters.com
www.faithwriters.com/conference.php

August: KARITOS CHRISTIAN ARTS CONFERENCE
Bolingbrook IL
Bob Hay
847-749-1284
bob@karitos.com
www.karitos.com

August : AMERICAN CHRISTIAN WRITERS
Dayton OH
Reg Forder
1-800-21-WRITE
ACWriters@aol.com
www.ACWriters.com

August: TEXAS CHRISTIAN WRITERS CONFERENCE
Houston TX
Martha Rogers
713-686-7209
marthalrogers@sbcglobal.net

August: GREATER PHILADELPHIA CHRISTIAN WRITERS CONFERENCE
Langhorne PA
Marlene Bagnull
610-626-6833
mbagnull@aol.com
www.writehisanswer.com/Philadelphia

August: THE WRITING ACADEMY SEMINAR
Minneapolis MN
Mar Korman
218-792-5144
jflz20@mcleodusa.net
www.wams.org/pages/2seminar.htm

August: AMERICAN CHRISTIAN WRITERS
Minneapolis MN
Reg Forder
1-800-21-WRITE
ACWriters@aol.com
www.ACWriters.com

August: AMERICAN CHRISTIAN WRITERS
Springfield MO
Reg Forder
1-800-21-WRITE
ACWriters@aol.com
www.ACWriters.com

August: CAPE COD SUMMER WRITERS CONFERENCE &
YOUNG WRITERS WORKSHOP (ages 12-16)
Oysterville MA
Jacqueline M. Loring
508-420-0200
writers@capecodwriterscenter.org
www.capecodwriterscenter.com

September: MARANATHA CHRISTIAN WRITERS CONFERENCE*
Muskegon MI
Verna Kokmeyer
www.WriteWithPurpose.org

September: NORTHWEST OHIO CHRISTIAN WRITERS CONFERENCE
Toledo OH
Linda Tippett Andamija@bex.net

September: SAN DIEGO CHRISTIAN WRITERS GUILD SEMINAR
San Diego CA
Robert & Jennie Gillespie
760-294-3269
info@sandiegocwg.org
www.sandiegocwg.org

September: INSCRIBE FALL CONFERENCE
Edmonton, Alberta, Canada
Director
780-542-7950
senappi@telusplanet.net
www.Inscribe.org

September: SILOAM SPRINGS WRITERS CONFERENCE
Siloam Springs AR
Rosemary M. Matthews
479-524-3506
Rosie1st2000@yahoo.com

September: NORTH TEXAS CHRISTIAN WRITERS CONFERENCE
Keller TX
Frank Ball
817-915-1688
frank.ball@ntchristianwriters.com
www.ntchristianwriters.com

September: AMERICAN CHRISTIAN WRITERS
Denver CO
Reg Forder
1-800-21-WRITE
ACWriters@aol.com
www.ACWriters.com

September: ACFW NATIONAL CONFERENCE
city unknown
ACFW Conference Committee
574-370-0988
pr@americanchristianfictionwriters.com
www.ACFW.com

September: AMERICAN CHRISTIAN WRITERS
Salt Lake City UT
Reg Forder
1-800-21-WRITE
ACWriters@aol.com
www.ACWriters.com

September: AMERICAN CHRISTIAN WRITERS
Spokane WA
Reg Forder
1-800-21-WRITE
ACWriters@aol.com
www.ACWriters.com

September: OKOBOJI CHRISTIAN WRITERS RETREAT
Okoboji IA
Denise Triggs,
Denise@waterfallmin.com
www.waterfallretreats.com

September -October: SANDY COVE CHRISTIAN WRITERS CONFERENCE
North East MD
Jim Watkins
800-234-2683
info@sandycove.org
www.sandycove.org/docs/writers.php

October: MY THOUGHT EXACTLY WRITERS RETREAT
Schuyler NE
Cheryl Paden
402-727-6508

October: CATCH THE WAVE WRITERS CONFERENCE
Woodstock GA
Cindy Simmons
770-928-2795
cynthiasimmons@christianauthorsguild.org
www.christianauthorsguild.org

October: INTERNATIONAL WRITERS FELLOWSHIP CONFERENCE
Brookville PA
Jan Sady
814 –856-2560
janfran@windstream.net

October: PEN TO PAPER LITERARY SYMPOSIUM
Dayton OH
Valerie Coleman
937-307-0760
info@penofthewriter.com
www.penofthewriter.com

October : SANTA BARBARA CHRISTIAN WRITERS CONFERENCE
Opal Mae Dailey
805-682-0316   opalmaedailey@aol.com

October: GLORIETA CHRISTIAN WRITERS CONFERENCE
CLASServices 505-899-4283
info@classervices.com   www.glorietaCWC.com

October: AMERICAN CHRISTIAN WRITERS
Anaheim CA
Reg Forder   1-800-21-WRITE;
ACWriters@aol.com   www.ACWriters.com

October: EARLHAM SCHOOL OF RELIGION/MINISTRY OF WRITING COLLOQUIUM
Richmond IN
Susan Yands   800-432-1377
yanossu@earlham.edu

October: WEST BRANCH CHRISTIAN WRITERS ONE-DAY CONFERENCE
Montoursville PA
Cindy Emmett Smith   Cswriter@yahoo.com

October: MOUNT HERMON MENTORING CLINIC
Mount Hermon CA (near Santa Cruz)
David Talbott   831-335-4466
rachelw@mhcamps.org
www.mounthermon.org/writersclinic

Oct: AMERICAN CHRISTIAN WRITERS
Phoenix AZ
Reg Forder   1-800-21-WRITE
ACWriters@aol.com
www.ACWriters.com

Early November: MINNESOTA CHRISTIAN WRITERS GUILD FALL SEMINAR
Minneapolis/St. Paul MN
Delores Topliff   651-695-0609
sharonknudson@hotmail.com
www.mnchristianwriters.org

November: HEART OF AMERICA FALL CONFERENCE
Kansas City MO
Mark Littleton
816-459-8016
HACWN@earthlink.net
www.hacwn.org

December: OAKWOOD COLLEGE CHRISTIAN WRITERS SEMINAR
Huntsville AL
Dr. Cecil Daly
256-852-8656
cdaly@oakwood.edu

Get Your Free Gifts Available at SynergyEnergyMarketing.com

Essence Magazine REPORTING STORES

In order to become an "Essence" best-seller, you must have a lot of books (hundreds) sold during a specified time period. The best way to sell a lot of books through the stores is to do a book tour and do a lot of promotion to drive people to the store to meet, greet and buy your book. *(note this is the current list at time of publication)*

1. Hood Books Headquarters (Detroit) (313) 515-7961
2. Mood Makers (Rochester, NY) (585) 271-7010
3. Precious Memories Bookstore (Richmond, VA) (804) 726-8501
4. Truth Bookstore (Southfield, MI) (248) 551-4824
5. Nu World of Books (Beaumont, Texas) (409) 838-2242
6. Pyramid Books (Florida) (561) 731-4422
7. Black Images Book Bazaar (Dallas, Texas) (214) 943-0142
8. African American Images (Chicago) (773) 445-0322
9. Kana's Cd's & Books (Columbus, OH) (614) 577-1897
10. Jokae's African American Books (Dallas), (214) 331-8100
11. Brownstone Books (Brooklyn, NY) (718) 953-7328
12. Knowledge Bookstore (Brampton, Ontario) (905) 459-9875
13. Shrine of the Black Madonna Bookstore (Detroit) (313) 491-0777
14. Black Classics Books and Gifts (Mobile, Alabama) (251) 476-1060
15. Cushcity.com (Houston, Texas) (281) 444-4265
16. Under One Roof (Killeen, Texas) (254) 554-6553
17. Alkebu-Lan Images (Nashville) (615) 321-4111
18. Shrine of the Black Madonna Bookstore (Houston, Tx) (713) 645-1071
19. Dynasty's Books (Charlotte, North Carolina), (704) 563-4520
20. Heritage Bookstore (Rancho Cucamonga, CA) (909) 484-8411

Get Your Free Gifts Available at SynergyEnergyMarketing.com

BOOK REVIEWER CONTACT INFORMATION

Send a short, concise cover letter requesting a review along with a copy of your book, a press release about your book, and a sales sheet.

The Wall Street Journal
Eric Gibson, Leisure & Arts Features Editor
200 Liberty St.
New York, NY 10281

Alternative Press Review
Columbia Alternative Library
PO Box 1446
Columbia MD 65205-1446

American Press Service & Features Syndicate
PO Box 917
Van Nuys, CA 91408

Kirkus Reviews
770 Broadway
New York, NY 10003

The New York Times Book Review
229 W. 43rd St.
New York, NY 10036

Small Press Review
P.O. Box 100
Paradise, CA 95967

Book Review Editor
Library Journal
360 Park Avenue South
New York, New York 10010

Hollywood Inside Syndicate
Attn: John Austin
P.O. Box 49957
Los Angeles, CA 90049-0957
non-fiction only

Booklist
American Library Association
50 E. Huron Chicago, IL 60611
Address your mailing to the appropriate individual using the information below:
    Adult Books: Brad Hooper, Adult Books Editor
    Books for Youth (Children's and YA): Stephanie Zvirin, Books for Youth Editor
    Reference Books: Mary Ellen Quinn, Reference Books Bulletin Editor

Gary Roen
Syndicated Reviewer
1600 Hull Circle
Orlando, FL 32806

American Book Review Unit for Contemporary Literature
Campus Box 4241
Illinois State University
Normal, IL 61790-4241

Book Talk JL Syndicate
399 NW 10th Court
Boca Raton, FL 33486

Newspaper Enterprise Association
200 Madison Ave, Floor 4
New York, NY 10016

Publishers Weekly
360 Park Avenue South
New York, NY 10010

Los Angeles Times Magazine
Times Mirror Square
Los Angeles, CA 90053

Foreword Magazine
Alex Moore, Managing Editor
129 1/2 East Front Street
Traverse City, MI 49684

James A. Cox
Editor-in-Chief
Midwest Book Review
278 Orchard Drive
Oregon, WI 53575

Submit two copies of your book, press release, and sale sheet to the School Library Journal if your book is appropriate for children and young adults.
SLJ
Attn: Trevelyn Jones
360 Park Avenue South, New York, NY 10010

Free Reviews for Independent and Self-Published Literature http://www.WordMyne.com
    http://www.getbookreviews.com/index.html
    http://www.bookreview.com/publishers2.htm

Get Your Free Gifts Available at SynergyEnergyMarketing.com

RECOMMENED READING FOR AUTHORS

1. *1001 Ways to Market Your Books* by John Kremer

2. *The Complete Guide to Book Publicity* by Jodee Blanco

3. *The Savvy Author's Guide to Book Publicity: A Comprehensive Resource--From Building the Buzz to Pitching the Press* by Lissa Warren

4. *Publicize Your Book!: An Insider's Guide to Getting Your Book the Attention It Deserves* by Jacqueline Deval

5. *Guerrilla Marketing for Writers : 100 Weapons to Help You Sell Your Work* by Jay Conrad Levinson, Rick Frishman, Michael Larsen

6. *Jump Start Your Book Sales: A Money-Making Guide for Authors, Independent Publishers and Small Presses* by Marilyn Ross, Tom Ross

7. *Start Small Finish BIG in Self Publishing* by Anthony Obey, Crystal Obey

8. *Complete Guide to Book Marketing* by David Cole

9. *A Simple Guide to Marketing Your Book: What an Author and Publisher Can Do to Sell More Books* by Mark Ortman

10. *Guerrilla Publicity: Hundreds of Sure-Fire Tactics to Get Maximum Sales for Minimum Dollars* by Jay Conrad Levinson, Rick Frishman, Jill Lublin

11. *Over 75 Good Ideas for Promoting Your Book* by Patricia L. Fry

12. *How To Publish and Promote Online* by M. J. Rose , Angela Adair-Hoy

Pick Up Your Own Copy of Each of These Books Today at SynergyEnergyMarketing.com

Get Your Free Gifts Available at SynergyEnergyMarketing.com

RECOMMENDED BOOKS FOR BUSINESS OWNERS

1. *Think and Grow Rich* - Napolean Hill

2. *How to Double Your Business Profits in 97 Days* - Robin J. Elliott

3. *How to Retire in One Year* - Robin J. Elliott

4. *The 4-Hour Workweek: Escape 9-5, Live Anywhere, and Join the New Rich* - Timothy Ferris

5. *How to Make Millions with Your Ideas: An Entrepreneur's Guide* – Dan S. Kennedy

6. *The Ultimate Marketing Plan: Find Your Hook. Communicate Your Message. Make Your Mark* – Dan S. Kennedy

7. *No B.S. Business Success and entire No B.S. book series* – Dan S. Kennedy

8. *Rich Dad, Poor Dad* – Robert T. Kiyosaki

9. *Cashflow Quadrant: Rich Dad's Guide to Financial Freedom* – Robert T. Kiyosaki

10. *Rich Dad's Guide to Investing* – Robert T. Kiyosaki

11. *The Slight Edge* – Jeff Olson

12. *The Warren Buffet Way* – Robert G. Hagstrom Bill Miller, and Ken Fisher

13. *The Real Warren Buffet: Managing Capital, Leading People* – James O'Loughlin

14. *The 21 Irrefutable Laws of Leadership* – John C. Maxwell

15. *The Upside of Adversity: Rising from the Pit to Greatness* – Os Hillman

16. *Refined by Fire: Defining Moments of Phenomenal Women* – Anthony and Crystal Obey

Pick Up Your Own Copy of Each of these Books Today at SynergyEnergyMarketing.com

Get Your Free Gifts Available at SynergyEnergyMarketing.com

WHO IS PAM PERRY?

The leading literary trade publication, *Publishers Weekly* called her a "PR Guru" and the *Detroit Free Press* described her as a "marketing whiz." She was recently awarded "Power Networker of the Year" by George Fraser in Detroit and given a "Woman of Excellence Award" from The Michigan Chronicle.

Known as the "connector," Pam Perry knows how to pull the right people together for the right project at the right time. Her public relations and advertising career spans over two decades. A graduate from Wayne State University with a B.A. in journalism, Perry has worked in media and the nonprofit sector.

She's had sales positions at the *Detroit Free Press*, WNIC FM and various advertising agencies working with clients like McDonalds and Ford Motor company. She's worked in fund raising and development –selling the vision and mission of Joy of Jesus and then The Salvation Army.

Perry was the founder of BART (Blacks in Advertising, Radio & Television), a nonprofit networking organization for African Americans in the media. Over a ten-year period, the organization hosted career conferences, award programs honoring African American heroes in the industry and held regular professional development meetings.

She is also a past winner of the "One to Watch" Award from the American Women in Radio and TV – Detroit Chapter and jointly won an Emmy for her work as a producer for "The Edge with Jeffrey Miller" television show. Currently she does public relations for the publishing industry and is a PR Coach for self-published Christian authors.

Her best training and experience came when she spent five years working in her husband's automotive marketing communications firm, PMG. Now she uses those skills to give back to ministries through Ministry Marketing Solutions which is a public relations/marketing consulting firm.

The website address is www.MinistryMarketingSolutions.com.

A consummate communicator, Perry has even taught journalism at Renaissance High School in Detroit . She also pens weekly columns in the *Michigan Chronicle* and *Michigan Front Page* on how to write a book, publish it, and promote it.

Her work has also appeared in *Gospel Today* magazine, *TheDetroit News*, *The Detroit Free Press*, *CBA Marketplace Magazine*, *Precious Times Magazine*, and *The Christian Communicator*.

Her passion is Christian books and assisting writers through the American Christian Writers Association (www.Acwriters.com) where she is president/founder of the Detroit Chapter. She and her family attend Life Changers Christian Center in Lansing under Drs. James and Stacia Pierce.

She and her husband, Marc have a daughter and live in the metro Detroit area. Perry can be reached at 248.426.2300 or via email at pamperry@ministrymarketingsolutions.com.

Get Your Free Gifts Available at SynergyEnergyMarketing.com

HOW CAN PAM PERRY HELP YOU?

- ✓ Do you want momentum in your marketing?
- ✓ Do you need someone to help you through the social media maze?
- ✓ Need Media Contacts?
- ✓ Want to "get out there?"
- ✓ Are you interested in making a huge shift for your success?
- ✓ Do you want personal results?

You Have 2 Choices!

1. Group Coaching

What is group coaching? Group Coaching is a terrific option to receive the benefits of public relations coaching in a group setting.

Sessions are held on Tuesdays and/or Thursdays evenings from 9:00pm - 10:00pm EST and the recordings are available if you can't make the teleclass.

We have 4 week, 8 week or 3 month programs.

This coaching is for anyone who wants a jumpstart on their book sales and increase brand equity.

Each session is complete with weekly objectives, accountability partners, goals, unlimited email coaching, and thirty minute sessions with me just to name a few.

To get the full details, email me at PamPerry@ministrymarketingsolutions.com

2. Individual PR Coaching

Coaching is the best way to get the strategic plan to make your dreams a reality.

Over the last few years my clients achieve tremendous success in their book projects and ministry.
In addition, my clients learned how to use Web 2.0 tools to brand, sold tons of books, became Essence bestsellers, received tons of speaking engagements, designed better marketing/branding materials, garnered massive exposure via print, radio and TV. I could go on but I won't – you get the picture.

What do you really want? I can help you. I understand Christian authors and I know what it takes to be a success in the literary market. Let me help you.

There are many plans available. Let's find the one that will work best for you. Shoot me an email and I'll send you an assessment form to see what your needs are and we'll get to work!

Or just visit: www.MinistryMarketingSolutions.com and fill out the form there.

Get Your Free Gifts Available at SynergyEnergyMarketing.com

WHO ARE ANTHONY & CRYSTAL OBEY?

Anthony and Crystal Obey are happily married business partners. They own a Direct Response Marketing & Copywriting business wherein they consult and write sales copy for small to mid-sized businesses to dramatically multiply the sales, profits, and effectiveness for their clients.

The Obeys use their elite-level certified consulting knowledge to plan, develop, and implement little known and highly effective marketing campaigns and strategies for businesses online, in print ads, and in direct mail. They help organizations double and quadruple their sales and profits by implementing lead generation campaigns, uncovering hidden profit sources, and lowering costs.

The Obeys are the publishers and compilers of the celebrated *Refined by Fire* Christian/Inspirational Women's book series and the authors of *Start Small Finish Big in Self-Publishing*. They also use their highly specialized marketing and packaging strategies to create and sell information products including audios, videos, and print products for targeted niche markets.

Anthony and Crystal are the Directors of *DollarMakers USA*; an international club of entrepreneurs and individuals who do Joint Ventures together, founded by Joint Venture expert, Robin J. Elliott. The Obeys use their Joint Venture savvy to advance their own business interests, help their consulting clients implement these strategies, and to create lucrative business partnerships with companies to market beneficial products and services to targeted niche markets.

Anthony and Crystal Obey are committed to following Jesus Christ and are using their business talents and insights to help people achieve their career and financial potential through best business and marketing practices.

For Free Information about how Copywriting, Publishing, and Marketing Services can grow your business visit www.PerfectStormConsulting.com

For Free Information about how Joint Ventures can grow your business and create passive income for you visit www.DollarMakersUSA.com

Get Your Free Gifts Available at SynergyEnergyMarketing.com

HOW CAN ANTHONY & CRYSTAL OBEY HELP YOU?

Anthony and Crystal would love to help you reach your goals as an author, entrepreneur, or organization. Here a few reasons why you may want to contact them today.

1. Anthony and Crystal are Direct Response Copywriters and Marketers who can help you with your online and offline lead generation campaigns, customer follow up, retention, and reactivation projects. They work internationally and can help you reach your goal of getting and keeping clients. **Contact them today for a Free Assessment (Valued at $297) to find out how they can best help you.**

2. Anthony and Crystal serve as the USA Country Directors for DollarMakers, an International Organization of Joint Venture Brokers, and can help you learn more about and implement joint ventures. The Obeys work with individuals, organizations, and businesses. **You can contact them today for more information, and visit their website for Free Audios, Videos, Articles, E Courses, and Ezines.**

3. Anthony and Crystal Obey Publish Information Products in Print, Audio, Video, and Digital Formats. **If you would like to work together on an information product for a particular niche, contact them today to discuss the possibilities.**

4. Anthony and Crystal Obey love setting up joint ventures, strategic alliances, and partnerships with people who understand the value, who are ethical people of integrity, and who want to do great things together. **If you have an idea about how you, or someone you know can partner with the Obeys, please contact the Obeys today to start a conversation about it.**

For Free Gifts and More Information About Copywriting, Publishing, and Marketing Go To www.PerfectStormConsulting.com

For Free Gifts and More Information About Joint Ventures Go To www.DollarMakersUSA.com

The Obeys are available for interviews and speaking engagements as their schedule permits. If you are interested please contact them today to check availability.

Special Note: if you have been inspired by something the Obeys said in this book please let them know because they love to meet other people who are reading and applying the information.

www.ingramcontent.com/pod-product-compliance
Lightning Source LLC
Chambersburg PA
CBHW081158180526
45170CB00006B/2133